Achieving Your Doctorate

While Working in Higher Education

T0354245

Sara Miller McCune founded SAGE Publishing in 1965 to support the dissemination of usable knowledge and educate a global community. SAGE publishes more than 1000 journals and over 800 new books each year, spanning a wide range of subject areas. Our growing selection of library products includes archives, data, case studies and video. SAGE remains majority owned by our founder and after her lifetime will become owned by a charitable trust that secures the company's continued independence.

Los Angeles | London | New Delhi | Singapore | Washington DC | Melbourne

Achieving Your Doctorate

While Working in Higher Education

Merryl Harvey and Barbara Howard-Hunt

Los Angeles | London | New Delhi
Singapore | Washington DC | Melbourne

Los Angeles | London | New Delhi
Singapore | Washington DC | Melbourne

SAGE Publications Ltd
1 Oliver's Yard
55 City Road
London EC1Y 1SP

SAGE Publications Inc.
2455 Teller Road
Thousand Oaks, California 91320

SAGE Publications India Pvt Ltd
B 1/I 1 Mohan Cooperative Industrial Area
Mathura Road
New Delhi 110 044

SAGE Publications Asia-Pacific Pte Ltd
3 Church Street
#10-04 Samsung Hub
Singapore 049483

Editor: Jai Seaman
Assistant editor: Charlotte Bush
Assistant editor, digital: Katherine Payne
Production editor: Martin Fox
Copyeditor: Sarah Bury
Proofreader: Brian McDowell
Indexer: Silvia Benvenuto
Marketing manager: Catherine Slinn
Cover design: Lisa Harper-Wells
Typeset by: C&M Digitals (P) Ltd, Chennai, India
Printed in the UK

Library of Congress Control Number: 2020950530

British Library Cataloguing in Publication data

A catalogue record for this book is available from the British Library

ISBN 978-1-5264-9912-7
ISBN 978-1-5264-9911-0 (pbk)

At SAGE we take sustainability seriously. Most of our products are printed in the UK using responsibly sourced papers and boards. When we print overseas we ensure sustainable papers are used as measured by the PREPS grading system. We undertake an annual audit to monitor our sustainability.

Contents

Extended contents

About the authors

Merryl Harvey qualified as a nurse in 1982 and a midwife in 1984 and took up an academic post at Birmingham City University in 1995. Merryl's PhD, which was completed in 2010, explored fathers' experiences of the birth and immediate care of their babies. Since that time, she has supervised PhD students to completion and supported the doctoral forum at Birmingham City University, Faculty of Health and Life Sciences. Merryl has a strong journal publication history. This includes a co-authored text on fatherhood in relation to midwifery and neonatal practice, published in 2012. She also co-authored *Research Methods for Nurses and Midwives* (Sage, 2017). A second edition is forthcoming. Merryl became Professor of Nursing and Family Health at Birmingham City University in 2017. Before her retirement in 2019, Merryl was co-lead of the Family Health Research Cluster and co-lead of the Elizabeth Bryan Multiple Births Centre. Since her retirement, Merryl has continued to supervise doctoral students.

Barbara Howard-Hunt is a medical anthropologist who has worked in academia since 1999. Much of her earlier work focused on student progression and academic development, where she developed a model of student academic development for the Faculty. Barbara's PhD, in which she explored the migration experiences of refugee Somali women, was completed in 2012. It was during this time that it became clear there was a need for a staff doctoral forum, which Barbara has now facilitated for several years. Barbara has worked extensively with colleagues, both in the UK and abroad, most recently in Zambia and Jamaica, to help them develop academically and professionally. Barbara currently supervises PhD students and has supervised a number of them to completion. She has published on the student experience and on marginalised communities, and is currently co-lead on a project concerned with inclusive practices within the Faculty of Health, Education and Life Sciences at Birmingham City University. Barbara has spoken nationally and internationally on the student experience, inclusivity, equality and diversity, and access to health care for marginalised communities. She is a member of the National Counselling Society.

Preface

We are delighted to be providing this book, and sincerely hope that you find it useful as you begin or continue your doctorate. We know that undertaking a part-time doctorate while working full-time in a lecturing role can be daunting. Despite the common ground shared with other groups of postgraduate research students, there are significant differences which are rarely discussed. We are aware that there are many excellent texts available on how to gain your PhD or Doctorate, and we do not want to replicate these.

If we visualise studying for a doctorate as a journey, it is useful to have a companion equipped with some knowledge, skills and strategies to make the journey just that little less troublesome. It is useful to journey alongside others who know something of the route you will undertake. They will have experience of the hills and valleys that must be navigated, where the sharp twists and turns are that can throw you off track and where you can draw upon your previous knowledge and skill-set, so that you can afford to cruise along at a slightly more leisurely pace. We offer this book as such a companion.

The nine chapters are arranged to map the route from the beginning to the end of the journey and beyond. We do this as we know that, for some, the journey will not end with the awarding of their doctorate and this can leave a significant void in their lives. With this in mind, suggestions are tentatively offered on how to navigate the 'afterwards', when the celebrations have died down and the question often asked is 'now what?' The chapters include a number of case studies, reflection stops and activities that will be helpful to you in steering your own route. We have kept the tone deliberately engaging and light, as we do not want to bore you, but to provide a companion that is both accessible and informative.

We hope the contents of this book, including the case studies, activities and other resources, will inspire, encourage, support and, when needed, empathise with you as you journey towards completion of your doctorate. We wholeheartedly believe that, in this book, there is something for everyone who is undertaking a doctorate or supporting those who are. We hope you enjoy using this book and wish you every success with your doctoral journey in whatever guise it takes.

Acknowledgements

We have learned much of what we know about undertaking a doctorate part-time, while working in a full-time teaching role, through our work with colleagues and students at Birmingham City University. We would personally like to thank all of our colleagues and students, both those in the United Kingdom and those further afield, for kindly giving us permission to use their experiences as case studies within this book. We would particularly like to thank all those colleagues who participated in the monthly doctoral forum. Without your participation and reflections, this book would not have been possible. We have learned so much from you. Finally, we would like to thank the editors and publishing team for their expert guidance and encouragement in preparing this book.

Online resources

Achieving Your Doctorate While Working in Higher Education is accompanied by a range of online resources to support you while you undertake a doctorate. These resources are available at: https://study.sagepub.com/harvey.

On the website you will find:

- **Templates and examples,** such as a blank personal development analysis, to give you practical, hands-on tools that you can use to map your own doctoral journey.
- **Weblinks** to help you find handy resources on a range of topics, from researching sources of funding to guidance on doing a viva.
- **Case studies** from over 20 postgraduate researchers enable you to explore the diversity of student experiences while studying for a doctorate.

One

Introduction: Setting the scene

This book is unusual in that it does not take a traditional approach to writing about a research degree. Its intention is not to provide guidance on issues such as choosing an appropriate research topic, methodological approach, or the intricacies of data collection and analysis. These aspects are all, of course, vital to a successful outcome for a doctorate, but are already covered extensively in other publications, such as Phillips and Pugh (2015), Petre and Rugg (2010) and Wisker (2008). Instead, this book is written exclusively from the perspective of those academics who are already established in their full-time higher education teaching roles and have undertaken, or are considering undertaking, doctoral study part-time. It offers an accessible and, we hope, engaging one-stop guide, which is positive yet realistic. It is written to be relevant from the very beginning of the doctoral journey right through to completion and the period afterwards.

We have tried to present the content of this book in as clear a format as possible. Our aim is to make it accessible to all styles of learners, from a broad range of backgrounds and disciplines, including our overseas colleagues. We have purposefully used a conversational style as we want to engage you as you read. We hope that you will stop for reflection at the various points within the chapters and participate in the guided activities we have provided, as they are relevant to you. If you would like more information or more practice on the various aspects of doctoral-level study, additional resources are provided on the book's online resources (https://study.sagepub.com/harvey). In presenting this book in the way that we have, we hope to encourage you to see the value of taking time to engage, time to reflect and time to talk to others. However you choose to engage with this book, our hope it that it will be a valuable resource to you.

Who are we?

Both authors are academics who have studied for a doctorate part-time while working full-time in academia. Professor Merryl Harvey is a nurse who undertook her part-time doctorate at a different university from the one in which she has worked for many years. Dr Barbara Howard-Hunt, a medical anthropologist, studied for her doctorate at the institution in which she works and was supervised by colleagues with whom she had a long, established professional relationship. Both can testify to the benefits and the limitations of undertaking a research degree while working full-time in their own or another institution. In addition to their own personal experiences, both authors have gained a wealth of insight, understanding and knowledge from facilitating the monthly doctoral forum over a period of years as well as supervising their own doctoral students, whose experience is reflected in many of the case studies in this book. Their experience will reflect the wider experience of other part-time doctoral students, who are the target audience of this book. It is these experiences that inform the contents of this book.

Why are we doing this?

We have long recognised that the experiences of part-time postgraduate students, who have an existing academic career and a full-time job, are fundamentally different from those of other groups of doctoral students. In the United Kingdom, most of this group are in employment within post-1992 universities, which, prior to gaining university status, were polytechnic institutions with a strong commitment to teaching and learning pedagogy rather than research. However, many of the academics employed at these newer higher education institutions (HEIs) are feeling pressured to study for a doctorate, which is often now a requirement for promotion. In addition to this, substantive quality assurance developments, such as the Higher Education Academy fellowships, which were introduced in 2003 to promote and celebrate excellence in teaching, mean that many academics would like recognition for their experience and professional development in teaching. Undertaking a doctorate is one way of achieving this.

The impetus for this book arose out of many discussions with colleagues during a monthly doctoral forum at our university, which was developed exclusively for staff who are already undertaking doctoral study in-house or elsewhere, or who are considering doing so in the near future. The forum was not open to other groups of doctoral students, such as Graduate Research Teaching Assistants (GRTAs) or other full-time postgraduate research students. Neither were postdocs or supervisors invited to attend. It was agreed that the latter group of postgraduate researchers have their own naturally-formed networks of support, such as breakfast journal clubs and seminars, which they can access to meet with their peers for mutual support. We know that these types of supportive peer groups can be enormously beneficial, helping postgraduate researchers to share research ideas, discuss research questions and give and receive feedback on each other's work.

This sharing of ideas and knowledge about procedures, systems and policies can also be crucial to students who may otherwise feel marginalised or isolated. In addition, and as pointed out by Wisker (2008), these kinds of peer-managed groups are also crucial in providing opportunities for the exploratory talk, which is absolutely essential to the development of ideas and the sharing of discoveries at the postgraduate level. Such networks can also facilitate the dissemination of skills and information, helping postgraduate students to keep in touch with each other and thereby providing emotional as well as practical support (Phillips and Pugh, 2015). Because these events often take place at the same time as teaching and other work, full-time academic staff who are also studying part-time for their doctorate often cannot avail themselves of such activities, due to the requirements of their jobs. The burden of work means that even when activities are arranged outside 'teaching' time, it can be difficult for them to attend.

The focus of the staff doctoral forum is to provide a safe, non-judgemental environment where everything 'doctoral' is open for discussion and there is usually no fixed agenda. However, on some occasions, attendees do decide what they want to discuss, and they select topics to explore and share together, such as 'Using the World Wide Web for Doctoral Study Work' or 'Top Tips when Arranging to Take a Sabbatical'. The forum takes place monthly, over a lunch-time period, for about one and a half hours. There is no requirement to attend every month and no pressure to stay for the entire meeting. It became apparent that these postgraduate research students welcomed such an environment, where nothing was off limits. They needed a space where they were entirely at liberty to tell it like it is, within a community where there is widely shared respect and an understanding of the pressures of time demands, increasing workloads and the difficult task of maintaining momentum and motivation.

While acknowledging the need for guidance around topics such as epistemology and conceptual frameworks, what became clear was that there was a pressing need for this group of postgraduate research students to be able to access some peer support. They needed a safe space to let their guard down and to be allowed to own up to the fact that they too, like the students they teach, may have a whole host of insecurities about their academic abilities, and at times feel extremely vulnerable. Proficient in the marking of coursework at undergraduate and master's level, many struggled with the demands of doctoral-level work. Other issues were also noted, such as the dreaded imposter syndrome and feelings of guilt and shame at being exposed as 'lacking' among their colleagues. Time pressures and constant workplace demands proved particularly stressful, when study days have to be cancelled to meet the needs of the department. This occurs most often at the request of line managers who need to prioritise tasks such as teaching, exam cover or marking.

There is also the potential for rivalry among colleagues who are not currently studying and may feel that it is unfair that their peers, undertaking doctoral-level study, may be granted protected study time, leaving them to complete work which would usually be shared. In addition, issues around power and hierarchy may be present. This can be especially troublesome when the supervisory team are also colleagues, and may in fact be in a junior position to those they are supervising through the doctoral journey. These issues and many more can cause a great deal of stress and anxiety, which are rooted in issues that the traditional research student is unlikely to encounter in the same way. We have been unable to find other textbooks on the market that consider these issues in any great depth from the perspective of the full-time academic lecturer studying for their own doctorate.

Why choose this book?

This book is written at a time of exciting change in the world of doctoral education, much of which is fuelled by an increased focus on research and a plethora of drivers, such as the Teaching Excellence and Student Outcomes Framework (Department of

Education, 2016). There is now also a greater number of ways in which a doctorate can be obtained, apart from the traditional PhD route. One result of this is greater participation rates in doctorate research education. In the academic year 2018/19, 77,965 people undertook doctoral research (Higher Education Student Statistics (HESA) 2020), with 23,920 of this number enrolled on a part-time basis. As we have said, a significant and increasing number of part-time doctoral students will be working full-time in academia and studying at the same time, a pattern that is replicated on an international basis. It is for all these postgraduate research students that this book is specifically written.

This book does not shy away from the politics, frustration and messiness of carrying out doctoral study, while working in the same or another HEI. It tells it as it is, warts and all, and makes no apology for its attention to the ancillary and softer issues that are important in considering the overall health and well-being of this group of postgraduate research students. This group of students often find themselves in a position of betwixt and between, being at the same time a full-time academic teacher and a part-time postgraduate research student. It is a path that is often difficult to navigate. In general, this book provides a light-hearted view on how to navigate the journey of doctoral study when already working as an academic, acknowledging that it can be difficult and emotional, especially for those who are already heavily invested in their academic careers. The aim of the book is always to provide critical insight based on the real-life experiences of people who have already gone through the process. This book should therefore be a valuable resource for this specific group of doctoral students as well as to other doctoral students, especially those who are undertaking part-time study.

Case studies

The case studies presented throughout the book are based on the experiences of one or more current or former postgraduate research students. Some case studies will feature only once and others will recur throughout the book. For example, the case study of Cora appears in most of the chapters. In order to protect their anonymity, and that of the institutions in which they work or study, all names in the case studies are fictional. However, everything reported will be a true reflection of the postgraduate research students' experiences.

Reflections and activities

Throughout the book there are opportunities to stop for reflection and to complete activities. The intention is to highlight areas for further reflection and, with exercises, to provide an opportunity for readers to consolidate what has been discussed in the chapter. The reader is also directed to other resources and reference points that should be helpful at the end of each chapter.

How this book is structured

Following this chapter, which sets the scene, there are eight subsequent chapters.

Chapter 2: What's driving you?

In this chapter attention is given to the motivators for undertaking doctoral-level study. The reader is encouraged to reflect on both intrinsic and extrinsic motivators and to consider whether it is the right time in their life for them to commit to undertaking doctoral-level study. A number of case studies are used to illustrate key points, such as being prepared to defend your decision to undertake doctoral-level study – why you should or should not do it. The chapter also provides an outline of the advantages and disadvantages of part-time doctoral study. It focuses on the many benefits for postgraduate research students who are already working in a university and culminates with a reflective activity that should be helpful in minimising the impact of the challenges inherent in any doctoral journey.

Chapter 3: Starting your journey

This chapter discusses the many decisions that the postgraduate research student has to make once they have decided to pursue doctoral-level study. It explores the benefits and limitations of studying in your own institution or one which is external to you. The case studies in this chapter are used to guide the reflective activities. We provide an overview of the main types of doctorate that are available and encourage the reader to weigh up the pros and cons of each of them in deciding which is the right one for them. The chapter ends by encouraging the reader to reflect on their own personal attributes in relation to where they will study and which type of doctorate is best suited to them.

Chapter 4: Transitioning to the doctorate experience

This chapter focuses on personal development planning and its significance for the postgraduate research student. It outlines why postgraduate research students need to take a personal development approach and signposts students to the myriad of useful online resources that are available, including the highly-acclaimed Research Development Framework. The reader is encouraged to set specific goals and to plan how they will achieve them. A number of resources are provided to help with this. We describe the reflective process in detail and how the reader can use it to monitor their progress.

Chapter 5: Supervision during your doctoral journey

In this chapter we encourage the reader to consider how they will develop and maintain a positive relationship with their supervisor(s). We help readers to think about how they will work with their supervisor(s) in a way that is supportive and facilitative, so that the roles and boundaries are clearly defined, which is a key consideration, especially when being supervised by someone you know. Strategies are suggested as to how to manage the supervisory relationship, taking into account hierarchies of power and the importance of recording the outcome of supervisory meetings. In this chapter the issue of remote or online supervision is also reviewed. A number of case studies and activities are provided to facilitate critical reflection on a range of scenarios concerning the supervisor/supervisee relationship, including when either the supervisor or student changes their place of employment.

Chapter 6: Navigating procedural challenges

This is the first of two chapters which identify the challenges encountered by many doctoral students, both procedural and personal. We would encourage you to read these chapters in conjunction with each other. In this chapter we concentrate on procedural and work-related factors that can present a barrier to progression. We offer advice on how to minimise the risks regarding those issues over which you have some degree of control and how best to manage those issues that are outside your remit. The case studies illustrate the experiences of postgraduate research students we have known, the challenges they have encountered and how these were overcome. The reflective activity encourages you to think about how you position yourself as a doctoral student, as this will influence how you manage your studies.

Chapter 7: Navigating personal and emotional challenges

While the focus of the previous chapter was on the procedural issues that can arise during the doctoral journey, in this chapter we consider the personal and emotional factors that can negatively impact on you and your progression. The chapter covers topics such as adjusting to the academic requirements of doctoral-level study and the need to hone any skills that you need to develop. Although this was the focus of Chapter 4, we also discuss it here to reinforce this very important issue for postgraduate research students. The chapter explores the issues of motivation and momentum, proposing strategies to help you when your enthusiasm and energy wane. The reflections and activities in this chapter are designed to encourage you to stop and think about your own well-being, any support that you may need and how to go about accessing it. We also cover the topic of the dreaded writer's block, and offer some suggestions as to what you can do when this occurs. The chapter concludes with an excerpt from one of our colleagues, who we think provides very sound advice.

Chapter 8: One stop to go: Preparing for thesis submission and the viva

This chapter details the finalisation of the thesis. It begins with a discussion on preparing for thesis submission and outlines some key considerations that will be helpful, especially if you are working to a tight deadline. We then consider the actual viva and how you can best prepare for this oral examination. Attention is then given to the selection of the examiners, taking into account that if you are studying at your employing institution, the internal examiner may be someone you know well. In this chapter we also offer some suggestions as to what you can reasonably expect to happen during the viva and how to conduct yourself when being examined.

Chapter 9: Arriving at your destination

In this final chapter we present the potential doctoral examination outcomes and discuss what each of them means. We look at how any one of these outcomes may impact on you, especially if, like the vast majority of doctoral candidates, you have amendments to make. Consideration is also given to life post-doctorate. We provide some activities that should help you to consider the direction in which you want to go at this stage. As with the other chapters, the structured reflections and activities should help to facilitate your thinking and, we hope, support you in making the decisions that are right for you.

Two

What's driving you?

Making the decision to pursue a doctorate is, we believe, fundamentally different for those already working in academia when compared to the conventional student embarking on a higher degree by research. The vast majority of this group of academics are employed in post-1992 universities which constitute around 47% of universities in the United Kingdom (Boliver, 2015). The reasons given for pursuing a doctorate are diverse as they are driven by a number of motivators, both intrinsic and extrinsic (Skakni, 2018).

This chapter aims to help you to consider your personal motivations for undertaking a postgraduate research degree. It is hoped that reading and reflecting on the contents of this chapter will help you to determine if you have the passion that is necessary to see you through the entire process of the doctoral journey, if this is what you decide to do. As well as personal motivators, you will be invited to consider other more extrinsic motivators: for example, current drivers within higher education, including the Research Excellence Framework (Higher Education Funding Council for England, 2009) and Teaching Excellence and Student Outcome Framework (Department for Education, 2016). Each of these frameworks embraces the notion of improving quality in teaching and research and a doctorate is seen as one important way of demonstrating and evidencing a level of expertise, and thus credibility, in these areas. You can access these frameworks via the book's online resources.

Intrinsic and extrinsic motivators

Career progression is often cited as a strong motivator for undertaking doctoral-level study (Skakni, 2018). Just as the number of those pursuing undergraduate study has risen over recent decades, so too has the number of postgraduates, and we have seen this increase represented in those seeking and gaining employment in universities. As younger staff with higher research degrees are employed within universities, those who already have an established career in academia but who have not undertaken a higher research degree may feel left behind.

This perception, to a large extent, has been generated over the years by the way in which many institutions have organised their research activity in silos, as though it is something that only a small number of staff can become involved in. This has left many academics feeling that research is outside their scope of practice and that it really is somebody else's business. Thankfully attitudes are now changing and there appears to be much more willingness on the part of research communities to invite others in. However, the legacy of the closed culture of research within some institutions has left many seasoned academics feeling out of their depth when it comes to research activity and therefore unsure that they would have anything meaningful to contribute. If you can associate with this or feel a little wobbly about your current level of knowledge in regards to research or research methodology, try not to worry too much. We would want you to be reassured that a lack of a sound grounding in research knowledge does not mean you are unsuitable for doctoral-level study. Remember that doing a doctorate is about 'learning' to do research and that most programmes begin with some form of research theory and skills training. Your supervisory team should help you with this. It may well be that in the run-up to actually starting your doctorate, you ask other doctoral students for ideas of what you could read to help you. The library staff and doctoral supervisors may also be able to help as they will know what the popular and current texts are for beginner doctoral students.

The challenge is that nowadays research activity is highly valued and promotion may well be dependent on an individual's willingness to undertake a research degree. Understandably, this can lead to feelings of insecurity among experienced academics who are not pursuing doctoral-level study, such as feeling that they have to continually justify their positions. These are powerful motivators, and we think they represent a dramatic change in the focus of post-1992 universities. These newer universities have traditionally competed in the marketplace based on their reputation for excellence in teaching and learning, rather than research. However, in recent years there seems to be a growing requirement for staff to excel in not only teaching but also research. A contributory factor is the need for universities to demonstrate their research capacity in order to attract funding. The number of doctoral students, including staff who are studying for a higher-level research degree or have completed a degree, is one way of evidencing this. The result is the continuing increase in full-time staff registering for a PhD, EdD or another type of doctorate. You may wish to visit the VITAE website for more information (www.vitae.ac.uk/). The VITAE website also signposts you to a series of short videos where different doctoral students share their own experiences of doctoral-level study. You might find it helpful to watch them. Each one is only a few minutes long. In Chapter 3 we have also summarised the different types of doctorate that are available in the UK. It is well worth looking at these as there may be some types of doctorate that you are not familiar with but which may just be right for you.

On a professional level, it is often hoped that gaining a doctorate will lead to promotion or a change in direction of career. In addition, more and more UK institutions are making a doctorate a prerequisite of the senior lecturer role. Someone who feels they are likely to have years ahead of them working in academia and are either currently working at this level or are hoping to secure promotion to this role, may think it wise to undertake a doctorate.

Whatever the drivers are, what is unquestionable is that there must be strong personal motivations for pursuing doctoral study. Superficial reasons, such as wanting the title because everyone else has it and not wanting to feel left behind, mean that the journey is likely to be fraught with difficulties. Without strong personal motivations and the desire to complete, success is likely to be an extreme challenge. We say this because it can be easy to get caught up in the bustle generated by the universities' desire to encourage staff to undertake a higher research degree. You must not allow this to distract your attention away from thinking through your personal motivations for embarking on such an intensive level of study. Personal motivators may include:

- Self-accomplishment
- The enjoyment and desire to learn
- Professional curiosity.

Activity 2.1

Make a list of your own personal motivators. Be completely honest.

Based on the list you have generated, if you were giving advice to a friend with the same list of motivators for undertaking doctoral study, what advice would you give to them?

Is the timing right?

Potential doctoral students often ask 'how much time does a doctorate take up of the average week', as if it were possible to give an exact figure, in hours, per week. We believe that trying to give precise figures is unhelpful and counterproductive as every individual works differently and of course there will be peaks and troughs during the journey. It is important that you are not deluded into thinking that undertaking a doctorate won't impact on your professional and personal life. It undoubtedly will.

This means that there is a need to analyse whether this is the right time in your life to commit to undertaking a higher degree by research. If there are things happening personally or professionally, now or in the near future, you will need to factor them into your plans. For example, do you plan a significant life event such as:

- Relationship change, separation or getting divorced
- Starting or adding to your family
- Changing employment or taking on a new professional role that will require a reconfiguration of your workload or responsibilities
- Moving house.

None of these necessarily means that you should not pursue doctoral study, but it would be wise to think through the likely impact of these events on your ability to engage with your studies while you are also working full-time. You are likely to find yourself under considerable time pressure and the process of undertaking doctoral study is never linear. You will also need to factor in any other commitments that you may have outside work and consider if you can balance these with the added pressure of doctoral study.

We are not suggesting that these issues are unique to academics, as time pressures are nearly always a challenge for postgraduate research students. However, it is our belief and experience that these issues are likely to be compounded and exacerbated for part-time postgraduate research students who are already working in academia full-time. There are some stark statistics which indicate that 66% of academics with mental health problems attribute these to work pressures (Metcalf et al., 2018). In the 2019 Postgraduate Researcher's Survey, Williams (2019) indicated that more than a quarter of respondents (26%) had considered leaving or interrupting their studies. Anxiety was a key feature in respondents' decision making which would suggest that postgraduate research students can experience very high levels of anxiety (Williams, 2019). In addition, Guthrie et al. (2017) have highlighted that more than 40% of postgraduate researchers report depression or stress-related problems. The increased work load associated with studying for a doctorate and the oft-reported imposter syndrome and self-doubt are commonly attributed to part-time postgraduate research students, including those who are already working full-time in higher education (Wisker, 2008). It is increasingly recognised that these feelings can trigger a situation which discourages individuals from seeking help even though they may be experiencing high levels of stress (Mills et al., 2014; Guthrie et al., 2017).

Forward planning is often the best strategy here and, if you know that you will face significant events, such as those listed above, it may be well worth considering putting off starting a doctorate until a later stage, as in the case of Peter.

Case study 2.1

Peter is a senior academic who became a parent a couple of years ago. The birth of his child was not straightforward and his daughter was born with some health problems that are ongoing. Peter has indicated that while he would like to undertake a doctorate at some time in the future, he realises that doing so now would place him under additional stress, and so has decided to put his plans for doctoral study on hold for the time being.

As discussed, starting the journey when you are already struggling with other considerable commitments is likely to lead to high levels of stress and a decrease in motivation.

Ask yourself...

What do you think of Peter's decision?

If you were in Peter's situation, would you have made a different choice?

If so, what reasons would you give?

We absolutely believe that there is no shame at all in saying, no, not now. In fact, quite the contrary, as this is a brave decision to make when everybody else seems to be jumping on the bus because it is the popular thing to do.

Of course, there are events for which we cannot plan, such as the Covid-19 pandemic, which is unfolding as we write this book. We are all having to adjust to very different ways of working and living, which means that some postgraduate research students have had to take an enforced break from their research for a variety of reasons. These include caring responsibilities or new work commitments. For example, many academic staff with a health professions background made the decision to return to the clinical area to help with the considerable strain that the National Health Service found itself under, while others helped with the production of personal protection equipment. Some researchers have encountered challenges associated with actually carrying out the research itself, such as gaining access to participants or subjects, and have either had to postpone that part of the work or instead modify what they had hoped to do. The latter course of action often requires resubmitting the research proposal to an ethics committee. While this current state of affairs could not have been predicted, it is good to plan for the unexpected so that when it does happen, you can meet that challenge from a position of strength rather than already having lots of things to worry about all at the same time.

It is also worth remembering that very many academics are successful in achieving their doctorates. Data show that 3,840 part-time doctoral students were successful in obtaining their doctorate in the academic year 2016/2017 (Higher Education Statistics Agency, 2018). We are sure that the vast majority of this number, although they may have had a challenging journey, will also have found the experience very satisfying and enjoyable.

Reflection 2.1

We would recommend that you seek out those in your circle who are currently studying or who have fairly recently achieved their own doctoral degree. It is always good to have the perspective of others, and to learn about their own reasons for undertaking a research degree. Try to seek insight from people you know, trust and respect, and absolutely avoid those who may be known for enjoying regaling their own 'horror' stories about their experiences. Do carefully consider the reasons some people give for you *not* to undertake a doctorate. You will need to consider carefully if they really do have your best interests at heart or if there may be other underlying reasons why they may wish to dissuade you.

We introduce the case study of Cora. Cora enjoyed a long-established career in academia as a senior lecturer and had successfully completed a number of projects when she decided the time was right for her to pursue a doctorate. You will read about her experience when she approached her line manager to gain support for her application to begin her doctorate. We will be returning to Cora's case study at various points throughout the book.

Case study 2.2

Cora was deciding whether to embark on a doctorate. Her family and friends were encouraging, as were some of her current and former colleagues. Cora raised the issue at her annual Performance Review but her line manager, Helen, was discouraging. Helen said Cora would find it too difficult, it would not benefit her career and that attaining a doctorate would also not benefit the team. Nevertheless, Cora pursued her doctorate. During the course of her studies, her line manager changed. Her new line manager was much more supportive and took every opportunity to offer encouragement. On completion of her doctorate, Cora reflected on many aspects of her experiences and remains hurt by the stance Helen took. However, Cora has rationalised this and now believes that Helen felt intimidated by the prospect of Cora working towards and achieving a doctorate.

Ask yourself...

Do you agree with Cora's summation of the likely cause of Helen's refusal to support her?

Are there other factors that could be at play here?

What would you do if you were faced with a similar situation? Who could you speak to in confidence?

It is useful to try to speak to different people, including those who are at different stages of the doctoral journey and, if at all possible, from a range of departments. Practice may differ in terms of how staff undertaking a doctorate are supported, or not, even within the same institution, and it is important not to be swayed by the view of a single individual.

Activity 2.2

Draw up a list of all the people you know who have completed or are undertaking doctoral-level study.

If you are struggling to do this, ask for help from the department responsible for doctoral research students in your institution, as they may be able to provide you with a list of names. If this is not possible, then it might be worth speaking to the Dean responsible for research within your faculty, department or school, or just ask around.

You can then select from this list those individuals you would like to approach. Set aside some time to meet with some or all of them. It might be useful to have a short list of questions to ask each person and to note down, either during or after the meeting, any salient points that you would wish to explore in more depth.

Reflection 2.2

If you are struggling to find time to do this initial exploration, you will need to consider how you will find time for the far more intensive doctorate-related tasks later on.

Having worked through, reflected on and discussed any issues raised from these meetings, you are now in a position to further analyse your reasons for wanting to undertake doctoral study. This might sound laboured but remember, it is likely to take between six and eight years of part-time study to achieve a doctorate. Therefore, beginning the journey is not for those without a strong will to succeed and if, like Cora, you find yourself with a less than supportive line manager, it is worth having your arguments prepared. You will need to be able to articulate how you plan to address any challenges you can anticipate.

Working through these activities will help with this. Your reflections will also be helpful if you need to pass an interview as a condition of being accepted onto a doctoral programme, as you will have already worked through many of the issues that your panel are likely to want to discuss. They will want to know that you have thought carefully about the commitment required for a doctorate as this will be a good indicator of your likelihood of successful completion.

Acknowledge your assets

Studying for a doctorate can result in an immense sense of intellectual satisfaction. As an academic, you may have spent years immersed in your discipline. It is a certainty that you will have a good knowledge of what works, what needs to be improved and may already have some well thought out ideas about how problems can be addressed within your field. This is a considerable advantage when planning the area of research you would like to undertake, as it is likely that the topic chosen will be closely related to the area of practice in which you are already working. You are therefore in a prime position to research topics that are of deep interest to you. As such, you are far more likely than other postgraduate research students to have a good idea of the focus of the research and will already have insight into what aspect of the topic it may or may not be possible to investigate for your doctorate.

Unlike other postgraduate researchers who may have little knowledge of the constraints of researching a particular issue, you are far more likely to be realistic about what can be done (Fillery-Travis and Robinson, 2018) and have the skills and knowledge to persuade your supervisory team of the focus of the research that you wish to pursue. Another key advantage is that you will also have some knowledge, to varying degrees, of the organisational structures and processes that may facilitate or hinder your research activity. If these are perceived to be challenging, you are in a prime position to explore what needs to happen to mitigate the challenges in the planning stages of the research. This can save you much angst and time later on as you progress with your research. In addition, it is highly probable that you will know, or at least be able to use your networks to find out, who should be able to help you either from within your own institution or from any discipline-specific organisations or networks in which you engage.

Another potential advantage of studying part-time while being employed full-time in higher education is the flexibility to combine other academic commitments, such as teaching, alongside pursuing an area of deep personal interest. At the same time, you will be maintaining a reliable income. You will read more about the financial implications of doctoral study in Chapter 3, where consideration is given to the potential benefits and limitations of undertaking doctoral-level study in your own institution. On another note, it is probable, as discussed earlier, that you will be researching in an area that you already know something about, so your personal motivation is likely to be substantial, especially as the end point is research that has the potential to have a significant impact within your own working environment. It is likely that your research will inform your own area of practice and maybe that of others within and outside your own institution. This can be enormously satisfying in terms of doing work that is enjoyable and that affords you the opportunity to develop real expertise within a particular area of practice.

Case study 2.3

Mercy completed a part-time doctorate at the institution in which she was employed full-time. After some time, she was looking for a change in the direction of her employment to something that was more challenging. Mercy started to look outside her institution as she was not aware of any internal opportunities, but she had little success. Some months later, a senior member of the management team, who had attended a presentation of Mercy's doctoral work, approached Mercy and said she was keen to invite Mercy to join her team to work on a specific project. The secondment subsequently became a permanent move, leading to much greater job satisfaction for Mercy.

Ask yourself...

Do you think it was pure luck that resulted in Mercy being approached by a senior manager?

What, if anything, would you have done differently and why?

Weighing it all up

A doctorate is a very individual experience, so undertaking an analysis of your strengths, weaknesses, opportunities and threats (SWOT) (Skills You Need, n.d.) can help you to recognise how you can turn any identified weaknesses into strengths and threats into opportunities. By investing time to think things through thoroughly, you will be giving yourself the best chance for success. You may also wish to discuss your thoughts with a trusted friend or colleague who can be relied upon to ask the awkward questions that you may be reluctant to delve into yourself. They may help you to consider things that you had not initially thought about but which could influence the actions you take. This is important, as you will need to maintain your motivation over a considerable period of time and it is easy to ignore or underestimate the commitment required to balance part-time doctoral study with a full-time academic job. It is essential that you therefore clear up any nagging doubts before you invest your time and money. As the old adage says, 'better a broken engagement than a broken marriage'. No one enjoys discontinuing their doctorate before they have completed. For academics who may be studying at their place of employment, there is the added level of stress associated with the loss of face among colleagues. Carrying out a thorough analysis of your SWOT can help you to identify any factors that could seriously

Goal: Developing my writing skills

Strengths	Weaknesses
• Determined • Good organisational skills • Highly motivated • Experience of writing at MSc level	• Imposter syndrome • Impatient • Fear of exposing lack of research or academic skills • Doing more of the same • Procrastination • Work–life balance
Opportunities	**Threats**
• Write something for publication • Join writing group • Improve information literacy and research skills • Enhance my self-esteem through learning • Promotes opportunity to evaluate my own performance, to identify my own learning needs and to ask for help	• Competing deadlines • Needs of the institution take priority • Supervisor's availability or lack of it • Access to required resources • Caring commitments

Strengths, or those areas where you have an advantage over others or some unique resources to draw on;

Weaknesses, or areas where you may be weaker than others and may find that others can do better than you;

Opportunities, or possibilities that you can take advantage of to help you achieve your goals and ambitions; and

Threats, or things that may prevent you from achieving your goals.

Figure 2.1 Example of a completed SWOT analysis

impact on your likelihood of completion, so that you are in a position to try to address them. Undertaking the reflection below can help you to really think through your reasons for exploring the possibility of studying at doctoral level and also what you hope to get out of it. You will find an example of a completed SWOT analysis in Figure 2.1. For more detail, go to the book's accompanying online resources.

Reflection 2.3

What do you hope to gain from undertaking your doctorate?

Why are you considering undertaking doctoral-level study and why at this time?

In essence, the reasons why individuals undertake doctoral-level study are diverse as they are driven by both personal needs and desires as well as a range of external factors. These reasons include:

- Improving career prospects
- Seeking personal development
- Boosting confidence
- Having an interest in a particular field of study
- The fear of getting left behind
- The expectation of the institution in which they are employed
- Wanting a challenge
- Wanting to do research
- To prove that they can do it
- As a means of maintaining motivation for their current role.

Reflection 2.4

What do you envisage you may miss out on by undertaking your doctorate?

How do you plan to minimise any identified challenges?

Table 2.1 is not an exhaustive list but summarises some of the advantages and disadvantages of studying for a doctorate. It reflects insights from current and former doctoral students. You may identify other advantages and disadvantages that are not listed. If you do, then write them down. Committing thoughts to paper can act as a useful *aide-mémoire*.

Table 2.1 The advantages and disadvantages of studying for a part-time doctorate

Advantages	Disadvantages
• Pursuing an area of research in which you have a deep interest • Making a unique contribution to the existing body of knowledge • Developing a wide range of skills, such as project planning, presentation skills, conceptual and analytical thinking, problem solving, writing for varied audiences • Becoming part of or establishing a network • Providing an opportunity for personal development • Boosting confidence and a sense of achievement • Recognising you have some expertise in a particular field • Career progression, such as a change of direction in your employment or an opportunity to secure your current role • Opportunities to disseminate research outside own institution • No break in service • Keeping a secure job and the salary that goes with it	• Maintaining motivation may be challenging • It is difficult to predict changes in personal circumstances over the length of a doctorate and to know how these may impact on your studies • Time pressure due to the commitments of reading, writing, collecting and analysing data etc. and how this competes with other academic commitments • Having to undertake further training and attend a structured induction course as part of the doctoral programme • Some colleagues may resent the fact that you are allocated time for study away from other academic commitments, such as teaching • No guarantee of career progression once completed • Long-term commitment but research interests may change over time • Having to make sacrifices, i.e. restricting social life or foregoing opportunities

It is also worth highlighting the less commonly discussed benefits of already working in academia. As someone who is already firmly established in their academic role, it can mean fairly easy access to colleagues, including those at a more senior level than yourself. Most people working within these areas are only too ready to help, considering it a compliment to be approached. The benefit of a short discussion, at an opportune moment, can be a considerable asset when help is needed, and one that you should not undervalue. From our own experience, we know that talking to someone who understands our concerns can make all the difference when important decisions are being made. It can be incredibly beneficial when a listening ear and clear head are needed to circumvent a particular problem or dilemma. A discussion with a trusted colleague, or a few encouraging words from them, especially if they have travelled the journey you are on, can help you to feel empowered and boost your self-esteem, especially if you are experiencing feelings of doubt about your ability to commit to undertaking doctoral-level study.

Planning ahead at this time can also be incredibly useful for later on, when you are actually studying, because if you are worried about something, there can be real benefits in not having to wait until your next supervisory meeting to discuss it. Sometimes these concerns may feel fairly trivial but nevertheless can be a worry, causing stress and anxiety, or the problem may relate to an issue with the supervisors themselves.

For these reasons, it is good practice to identify, early on, who your doctoral 'buddies' are and how you will work together.

We are aware that discussion in this chapter could be perceived to be focused more on the negatives, rather than the positives, of undertaking a doctorate and may have provoked some mild anxiety. This is not our intention, and we do hope that thinking through some of the points discussed above will be helpful to you rather than off-putting. As we have said in our introduction to this book, we aim to tell it warts and all, without scaremongering.

Working through these activities, and taking the time to stop and think through the points of reflection, when guided, we hope will be helpful to you. There is no shame in coming to the realisation that starting a doctorate may not be the right thing for you to do at this time and that it may be better to defer for a couple of years. As we have said, it is better to decide not to begin doctoral-level study than to start and then run into difficulties that were predictable. Postgraduate study at doctorate level is not for everyone, and there are other ways of developing your interest in a particular area, such as by writing a report or a position piece for a journal or a book, or undertaking a small-scale research project. There may also be other ways of facilitating career progression within the institution by engaging in other roles or activities that do not require the same degree of determination, resilience and institutional regulations as those involved in doctoral study.

Think back to the case study of Mercy, who may have had the same outcome if she had made it known what her aspirations were.

Having thought things through, you should discuss your plans with your line manager. A good time to do this may be during your annual performance review. You may receive the response you had hoped for, or even be pleasantly surprised, but do remember the case study of Cora and be prepared to defend your case, if you meet with a great deal of resistance.

There is no doubt that despite its ups and downs, doctoral study can be immensely satisfying and enjoyable, with many people describing it as the best thing they have ever done, us included. The case study of Pnina below illustrates the experiences of a former postgraduate research student and may offer some further insight into the reality of doctoral study for academics. We believe it captures the highs and lows of the journey particularly well.

Case study 2.4

Pnina is an experienced higher education senior lecturer who completed her undergraduate degree and subsequent full-time Master's degree as a mature student. She has worked at her employing institution, a post-1992 higher education institution, for just over 20 years. During that time, she has worked in a number of roles, some of which meant that she was actively

(Continued)

involved in research. She enrolled for a doctorate, with much trepidation, having always believed that she couldn't possibly achieve a PhD, but excited at the prospect that it may one day be a reality for her. Her reasons for undertaking doctoral study were primarily her passion for the subject and because she wanted to continue researching as she enjoyed it and was highly motivated. She did not have particularly clear career aspirations, but was simply thrilled to have the opportunity to pursue a doctorate in her employing institution.

She had invested a significant amount of time and energy, thinking through and developing her research question, methodological approach and deciding who would be best approached to supervise her. However far less time was spent on thinking through other important aspects of the doctoral journey, such as who her support network would be. This had serious implications as she often felt marginalised, with nobody to speak to, as little worries developed into big fears and anxieties. At the time she was studying, there were very few other part-time postgraduate research students at her institution and even fewer who were also working full-time as well. Neither had she given much thought to the difficulties of combining part-time study, of which she had no previous experience, with a demanding full-time job, believing somehow that she would be able to manage both.

A lack of supportive networks meant that she tended to rely heavily on her supervisors for emotional as well as academic assistance. She had not anticipated the big step up from MSc study to doctoral-level study. Neither had she appreciated just how much autonomy there would be, as it was Pnina herself who had to steer her own ship, so to speak. At several points throughout the journey, having not made the progress she had anticipated, she had felt that the best thing to do was to withdraw. She came to believe that she simply did not have the skills required for such labour-intensive and intellectually demanding work. Instead, she felt that she was an imposter. She experienced strong feelings of shame and guilt, believing she was letting everyone down.

However, she persisted in her studies, facing some significant life events along the way, including the death of both parents, becoming a grandparent for the first time and remarrying. Her sheer determination not to give in, coupled with her enthusiasm for the topic of study and the support of her supervisors and line manager, meant she limped, as it were, to the finishing line. Well, she describes the end as being more like a sprint, due to the fast-approaching deadline. She managed to submit her thesis just in time, which, after a successful and enjoyable viva and some moderations, was deemed of a good enough standard for her to be awarded her PhD. Some months later she progressed into a more research-focused role at her institution which she is thoroughly enjoying.

Ask yourself...

Are there any particular elements of Pnina's story that specifically speak to you?

In regards to planning ahead, is there anything that you could be doing now that may help you to navigate your way through the doctoral journey and minimise some of the anxieties Pnina faced?

Things we have thought about that may have been helpful to Pnina include:

- Making sure you have a good supportive network around you and have agreed how and when you can contact them

- Identifying any gaps in your skill-set and working out how and when you will address them
- Mapping out the peaks and troughs in your work-flow so that you can most effectively make use of any study time allocated
- Devising a good study plan, but allowing for some flexibility when needed
- Planning in breaks throughout the academic year and making sure you take them so that you can recharge your batteries
- Investigating the possibility of a sabbatical and planning when would the best time to take it.

If you have made the decision to begin doctoral study, we hope that the reflective activities in this chapter will help to make your journey just that little less eventful and that you will avoid some of the pitfalls associated with a lack of support and not planning ahead. As we have said, having people around you, who believe in you, can be motivational and empowering. They can help you to develop and use the problem-solving skills required to meet the challenges you may encounter. We would argue that this is vital for most postgraduate research students. Having this support and planning forward will mean that you can approach your doctoral studies with the enthusiasm, determination and self-confidence that signals success.

Our advice to those considering undertaking a doctorate is:

- To consider carefully if you have the motivation, determination and resilience required
- To work out the benefits and limitations for you of undertaking doctoral-level study
- To decide if you would prefer to enrol at your own institution or another one, and if the latter, what support you can expect from your own institution
- To speak to as many people as possible about their experiences of part-time doctoral study while working full-time
- To make a plan of how you will manage your work life, family life and your studies
- To speak to your line manager and work out together what allowances can be made for study time and how this will work in practice, taking into account the peaks and ebbs of the academic year
- To work out who your local network of support will be and speak to them about your plans. If possible, identify a peer who you can call on without notice and who you can agree to meet up with on a regular basis
- To connect to any forums or networks, either within or outside your own institution, and make a plan of how you will be able to access them (this may be remotely).

In conclusion, it is hoped that this chapter has helped you to analyse your answers to the questions: 'Why do I want to get into the driving seat of doctoral-level study?' 'And why now?' We do hope that this discussion helps to highlight the reality of what is required in order to achieve a doctorate without being overly pessimistic. We believe that time spent reflecting on the issues raised can help to reduce anxiety and save much angst later on in the journey when the passion for studying has waned and what is needed is a clear focus, hard work, persistence, determination and a great deal of resilience. If you have read this far and still feel very passionate about undertaking a doctorate, then you should not doubt that you have the attributes necessary to see you through the journey to the final destination of gaining your doctoral degree.

> To access the online resources accompanying this chapter, please visit:
> https://study.sagepub.com/harvey

Three

Starting your journey

Having decided to undertake a doctorate, there are other decisions that you need to make before you can get started. In this chapter, we explore deciding where you will undertake your doctorate. The premise of this book is academics undertaking a part-time doctorate in their home institution. However, we will also consider the potential implications of other options that are available to you. The various routes to gaining a doctorate are then examined. This includes looking at the benefits and possible limitations of the various different types of doctorate. Case studies are used to illustrate academics' experiences of the different doctoral options. Activities are suggested that we hope will enable you to make the decision that is right for you. Supplementary questions to consider before making your decision are signposted on the book's online resources.

Decisions about your doctorate

The doctoral landscape has changed considerably over the last decade (Wildy et al., 2015; Rees et al., 2019). While some disciplines have a long-standing doctoral tradition, for others it is relatively new. In recent times, there has also been an increase in the different types of doctorate available and the number of institutions offering this level of study (Lee et al., 2012; Volkert et al., 2018). Anyone embarking on a doctorate has important decisions to make and these are no easier if you are already working in academia. Indeed, that can bring its own challenges. This is because decisions must be made in the context of your other academic responsibilities, the expectations of your home institution and the proposed focus of your doctorate. Deciding on the type of doctorate, academic institution and the timeframe (full- or part-time study)

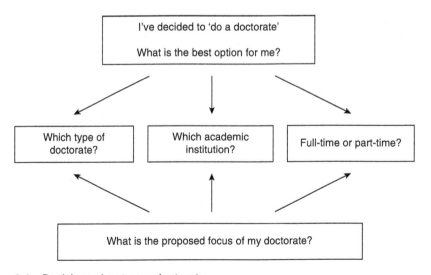

Figure 3.1 Decisions about your doctorate

are therefore integral elements to making the overall decision to do a doctorate (see Figure 3.1). Making these decisions is not a linear process. All factors will probably be influential, although some may be more important to you than others.

Home or away?

It must be acknowledged that academic snobbery persists in some quarters regarding the institution where a doctorate is undertaken (Pástor and Wakeling, 2018). This notion is more prevalent in some disciplines than in others and may, in turn, affect longer-term career projection (Pástor and Wakeling, 2018). While this may influence your choice of institution, many academics enrol within the institutions in which they are employed. Conversely, others may make the decision to study elsewhere for a variety of reasons. There is no right or wrong decision here. Each person should make the decision that they consider to be the most appropriate for them. However, we acknowledge that for an academic, the options in terms of 'home or away', type of doctorate, timeframe and the proposed focus may be more limited. You should therefore establish what choices you have at the outset. Otherwise, you risk spending time and energy exploring perceived options that are not in fact available to you.

If you do have a choice regarding 'home or away', the question to ask yourself is 'Should I undertake the doctorate in my home institution?' The following activity will hopefully help you to reach the right decision for you.

Activity 3.1

Identify the benefits and disadvantages to *you* of doing your doctorate in your home institution or in an external institution.

Here are our thoughts:

1   Possible benefits of undertaking a doctorate in your home institution:

- Doctoral funding may be prioritised for those studying in-house. It may be the only way that you can secure internal funding to do a doctorate.
- Doctoral funding may be prioritised on areas of research which closely align to the institution's vision. It may be the only way that you can secure internal funding to do a doctorate.
- The range of doctorates on offer fit with your preferred type of doctorate.
- Your proposed doctoral topic fits with subject specialism within the institution.
- Your proposed doctoral study fits with research-methods specialism within the institution.

- You know something about the research activity of the organisation and how your own area of interest may align with that of the department, faculty or institution.
- You have identified potential supervisors who have subject and/or research methods specialist knowledge appropriate to your proposed topic.
- Supervision and other doctorate-related activities will be readily accessible.
- Potential supervisors are already known to you and you feel this will be an advantage. You will not have to invest time and effort in developing a trusting working relationship.
- Supervision can be fitted in around your workload and that of your supervisors.
- You have already established an academic and/or professional identity within the institution and you feel this will be an advantage.
- You will have easy access to resources, for example, specialist recording equipment, software programs and printing.
- You will have easy access to staff who can provide specialist services, such as information technology or information literacy.

2 Possible benefits of undertaking a doctorate in an external institution:

- The range of doctorates on offer fit with your preference of doctoral type.
- Your proposed doctoral topic fits with a subject specialism within the institution.
- Your proposed doctoral study fits with a research-methods specialism within the institution.
- It will enable you to keep a clear distinction between your place of work and place of study.
- Travel time to supervision and other doctoral activities will provide 'head-space' for you to think.
- The external institution will provide you with exposure to new people (supervisors, lecturers, students) and new ways of thinking, working and networking.
- Potential supervisors are not previously known to you and you feel this will be an advantage.
- Attending supervision, doctoral activities and travel time will be protected because they will be built into your schedule. This will provide legitimate time away from the demands of your academic role.
- You are unknown to lecturers, those who provide specialist services and students at the external institution and you feel this will be an advantage.

3 Possible disadvantages of undertaking a doctorate in your home institution:

- The range of doctorates on offer does not fit with your preferred type of doctorate.
- Your proposed doctoral topic does not fit with subject specialisms within the institution.
- Your proposed doctoral study does not fit with a research-methods specialism within the institution.
- You would not benefit from the 'head-space' that you would have in the travel time to or from an external institution.
- Suitable or appropriate supervisors are not available at your place of work and the institution will not facilitate the appointment of a more appropriate external supervisor or expert as part of your supervisory team.
- Potential supervisors are already known to you and you feel this would be a disadvantage.

- You feel you would not benefit from exposure to new people (supervisors, lecturers, students) and new ways of thinking, working and networking afforded by an external institution.
- Time to attend supervision and doctoral activities may be less protected because you or your supervisor(s) may be pulled back into the institution's activity.
- You have already established an academic or professional identity within the institution and you feel this would be a disadvantage.
- There is nowhere to hide on occasions when you may feel the need to, for example when deadlines are fast approaching or have been missed, when things go wrong or when you need space and time away from your studies.
- It may be more likely that you will be pulled in to cover the needs of the department because you will be more accessible than doctoral students who are off-site while attending an external institution.

4   Possible disadvantages of undertaking a doctorate in an external institution:

- Your institution will not fund you to undertake a doctorate at an external institution. In order to do this, you will either have to self-fund or secure external funding.
- The range of doctorates on offer does not fit with your preferred type of doctorate.
- Your proposed doctoral topic does not fit with subject specialisms within the institution.
- Your proposed doctoral study does not fit with a research-methods specialism within the institution.
- Accommodating supervision and travel time may be problematic.
- Potential supervisors are unknown to you and you feel this could be a disadvantage.
- The cost to you of the time and expense to attend supervision and other doctorate-related activities may be too great.
- You are not known to your supervisors, lecturers or students and you feel this could be a disadvantage.
- You may need to purchase resources, such as software packages or specialist recording equipment, if these are not available at the external institution. While you may be able to apply for funding to cover these expenses, making such an application may be time-consuming and ultimately unsuccessful.
- It may take time to establish relationships with staff who can provide specialist services, for example, information technology or library services.
- Obtaining support from specialist services may be problematic if face-to-face support is only available at times that you are unable to attend.
- It may take time to understand the external institution's processes, procedures and general ways of working, which may initially delay your doctoral progress.

We have suggested the potential benefits and disadvantages of doing a doctorate in your home or an external institution. Not all of these are likely to apply to your situation and you may have identified others that we have not included. Irrespective of the other pros and cons, for many academics, funding is the overriding factor. This is why it features so highly above. Increasingly, the only way for academics to secure internal funding is to do their doctorate in their home institution. Primarily because of financial constraints, some institutions are becoming less likely to fund an external doctorate. However, you may be able to put together a good case for funding an external doctorate, particularly if it is based on the subject, research-method specialism or supervisor expertise that only an external institution can provide.

Note that institutions will have different processes and procedures that could impact on the decisions you make about whether to undertake your doctorate at 'home' or 'away'. For example, as we will see in Chapter 5, some doctoral students have no say in the allocation of their supervisors. Therefore, be careful about basing your decision to undertake your doctorate in your home institution entirely on your preferred choice of supervisor. You may end up being disappointed.

If you are considering undertaking your doctorate at an external institution, remember that you may need to attend taught modules and other doctoral activities in addition to supervisory meetings. Distance-learning and the use of social media can often override the need to attend the institution on a regular basis. However, there may still be occasions where you need to attend face-to-face events or seek support from specialist services. Indeed, some institutions will require students to attend a minimum amount of time on campus. You should therefore find out the external institution's expectations regarding attendance and what your institution's position is on travel time. Is travel time included in your allocation of study time or do you have to add on this time? Will the cost of your travel expenses be covered? Do not assume anything; rather, ensure that you have all the information that you need in writing (or at least confirmed by email) to furnish your decision.

In making your decision, do not be swayed by the decisions made by your friends and colleagues. Only you can identify what is right for you. Having said this, some people do change institution part way through their doctorate. This may be because they have changed their place of work or because they feel the initial institution is not meeting their needs. Changing institution can be quite a bureaucratic process, and fraught with anxiety. However, for some doctoral students it is the best thing for them to do. Changing institutions part-way through a doctorate will be explored in more detail in Chapter 5.

If you decide, for whatever reasons, to undertake your doctorate in your home institution, we feel it is important that you are aware at the outset of some of the advantages and disadvantages that we have identified. This knowledge will enable you to be more proactive in attempting to address the disadvantages or potential pitfalls. We advocate discussing these advantages and disadvantages with your supervisory team at the outset and, where appropriate, develop an action plan to put strategies in place. We will explore in more detail potential strategies to address these challenges in Chapters 5, 6 and 7.

In deciding whether to undertake your doctorate 'home' or 'away', we offer two contrasting case studies, aspects of which, may relate to you.

Case study 3.1

Raymond decided to undertake his doctorate at his home institution. He assumed that the academic and personal support he would receive would be at least equivalent to that provided by other institutions. Raymond also felt that with a full academic load, the travel time to an external institution would be an unnecessary burden for him. Additionally, he felt that more direct access to his supervisory team and academic resources would be beneficial to him. Although at the time he embarked on his doctorate his home institution would have potentially funded studying at an external institution, he was aware that this was becoming increasingly difficult for other doctoral students to secure.

Case study 3.2

Cora decided to undertake her doctorate at an external institution. While this decision was primarily based on the subject-specialist knowledge at the external institution, she also felt that being unknown in that university would enable her to be herself. This would therefore remove any 'baggage' associated with studying for her doctorate at her home institution. The external institution was within walking distance of her place of work. Cora had sufficient control over her diary to be able to build-in walking time without compromising her allocated study time. She therefore lengthened her working day to compensate for the time she spent walking to and from the external institution.

Full-time or part-time?

Having addressed 'which academic institution?' (Figure 3.1), deciding on the time-frame (full- or part-time study) must be considered in the context of your current situation, subject area and potential topic. In almost all cases, academics undertaking a doctorate do so on a part-time basis. Very few funding opportunities are available within institutions for academics to support full-time study. However, it may be worth exploring the possibility of full-time study for at least part of your doctorate. Find out what opportunities are available at your institution. Sometimes these are not widely advertised, so you have to ask. While some external funding is available to support full-time doctorates, it is usually specific to particular disciplines and you will need to secure support from your home institution before applying (for examples, see the online resources). In some instances, it is the institution that has to apply, rather than the individual. Consult colleagues, subject specialists and professional bodies about potential sources of funding that may be available to you. If you are able to secure full-time funding, we recommend that you should be cautious about any permanent change to your contract that may jeopardise your role within the institution in the longer term. Therefore, seek guidance from your line manager, the Human Resources department and, if appropriate, from your professional body in order to ensure that your longer-term employment within the organisation is secure.

The timeframe for most academics undertaking a part-time doctorate is six to eight years, as determined by the specific programme of study and the institution. However, it may be possible to secure internal or external funding or a bursary at some point for a sabbatical in order to focus, for example, on data collection, data analysis or thesis writing (for examples, see the online resources). Your institution should make you aware of internal funding opportunities, but it is always worth asking whether they are available and to explore the application criteria. Taking sabbaticals is considered in more detail in Chapter 7.

Case study 3.3

Alfredia is a senior lecturer. The faculty where she works has a policy whereby academics can apply for funding for a six-month sabbatical to support writing up their doctoral thesis. Certain checks and balances are in place, so this support is not guaranteed. One of the factors influencing the allocation of funding is the student's progress to date. Alfredia was mindful of this during the early part of her doctorate and this was one of the motivators that kept her 'on track'.

What type of doctorate?

If you are undertaking your doctorate in your home institution, you will inevitably be constrained by the types of doctorate that are available. The options may include a PhD by research, a professional doctorate or a PhD by publication. If you have a choice, deciding which doctorate to undertake could be influenced by your area of interest, longer-term career plans, preferred mode of study and your academic activity to date. Myths and misconceptions exist about the different types of doctorate and these are often based on misguided perceptions of academic kudos (Birks and Watson, 2018). These opinions may knowingly or unwittingly impact upon the decisions you might make about which type of doctorate to pursue. In the following section, we will explore the different types of doctorate and we aim to give a balanced view.

PhD by research

This has been the traditional research-based doctorate and is considered by many to be the 'gold standard' (Birks and Watson, 2018). As the name suggests, the focus of this doctorate is a research study (or several smaller interconnected studies) culminating in the production of a thesis usually of 80–100,000 words. The institution where the doctorate is undertaken must formally approve the topic before the research can begin. However, the student can be less constrained in their choice than they would be if they were undertaking a professional doctorate (see below). Depending on the student's background or the requirements of the institution, there may be an assessed component at the beginning of the PhD (for example, Postgraduate Certificate in Research or an in-house assessed programme). From that point on, the student will probably be required to produce academic work for progression assessment. They may also work on draft chapters, conference presentations and papers for publication, and further progression assessment during the doctorate. Nevertheless, it can be a less structured programme. This means there are more limited formal opportunities for students to receive feedback on the development of their academic writing.

If there is a taught component at the start of the doctorate, this will place the student in a cohort which could potentially provide ongoing support throughout the doctorate. A PhD may also be undertaken as part of a larger programme of research, which will mean the student has contact with other members of the team. However, most students undertaking a PhD by research do so in isolation. This does not suit everyone and those undertaking a part-time PhD can feel particularly lonely. The less structured approach may also mean that some academics find it difficult to take the allocated study time to which they are entitled. Key elements of the research, such as participant recruitment and data collection, may also clash with peaks in the student's academic workload.

Case study 3.4

Parveen attended the Postgraduate Certificate in Research at the beginning of her part-time doctorate in her home institution. This placed her in a cohort of academics from across the institution. Over the length of her doctorate, she found the support provided by her fellow students invaluable. They used social media to keep in contact and met up periodically. Through this contact Parveen gained an understanding of the needs and challenges faced by colleagues working in other disciplines. She also learned about the different research methods and strategies they were utilising, some of which she made use of herself.

Case study 3.5

Cora was not required to attend the taught component of the doctorate she was undertaking at an external institution. She secured academic credit for her prior research activity. In some respects, this meant Cora was more isolated than other doctoral students at the institution. Her supervisory team was concerned about this and ensured that she was invited to relevant

(Continued)

research-related meetings and events. Cora attended the events that she could, but this was difficult to build into her schedule. Cora's supervisory team endeavoured to secure her a desk to use in the research office, in the hope that it would enable her to network with other researchers at the institution. However, this never materialised. Cora was nevertheless unconcerned about being isolated. Indeed, it suited her as she felt that she was able to focus completely on her doctorate without distractions.

Professional doctorate

This doctorate is discipline-specific and is more established in some professions than in others. Among the most recognised and long-standing are the Doctor of Education (EdD) and the Doctor of Business Administration (DBA) (Wildy et al., 2015). The professional doctorate may be particularly suited to those who feel their future career will be focused within the profession or discipline allied to the doctorate. Some academic institutions may also prefer their staff to undertake a professional doctorate. This type of programme usually contains taught or coursework-based components, linked to specific academic assessment. The requirement to attend sessions may make it easier for an academic to ensure that they take their allocated study time. Although there is a research component at the end of the doctorate, this is smaller than that of the PhD by research, and usually culminates in a thesis of 30–50,000 words. The focus of the research must conform with that of the discipline of the doctorate. Some students may therefore feel more confined in terms of their choice of topic or focus.

The professional doctorate can provide a more structured approach than other types of PhD. For those working part-time, this can be a more manageable approach to doing a doctorate. There may be scope to forward plan and negotiate future workload to coincide with the taught and coursework elements and the submission of assignments. Feedback from assignment work can also provide a benchmark for the requirements of doctoral study. In addition, the taught component places the student within a cohort for at least part of the doctorate, allowing them to share ideas and support in what can otherwise be a lonely journey, particularly through a part-time doctorate.

Case study 3.6

Marcus had worked in academia for six years. He now felt the time was right for him to commence a doctorate. He anticipated that his career would be focused in his discipline within academia for the foreseeable future. Marcus elected to undertake a professional doctorate. He felt that the programme of study would be in more manageable chunks for him. He also felt that feedback from individual assignments would enable him to achieve the required doctoral level of study. Additionally, in his discipline, the professional doctorate was more highly valued than the PhD by research.

PhD by publication

These doctorates are awarded based on a series of distinct, peer-reviewed, published, research-related papers that are authored or co-authored by the student (Jackson, 2013; Rees et al., 2019). The doctorate can be based on publications that are retrospective (work already published) or prospective (work in development at the time that the doctorate is commenced) (Peacock, 2017). The increasing profile of this type of doctorate has coincided with the drive to increase the publication of research (Peacock, 2017; Birks and Watson, 2018). For those who are already published, or who know that they will be working on papers, a PhD by publication may seem the obvious choice – why reinvent the wheel? The prospective PhD by publication is particularly suited to someone who has worked (or is currently working) on projects or studies from which there will be future publications. There are other benefits of this type of doctorate, including the prompt dissemination of research findings and the development of a research/publication track record sooner than for those taking alternative doctoral routes. This could, in turn, support swifter career development and promotion, and could contribute to the Research Exercise Framework (REF) assessment compared to other doctoral routes (Lee et al., 2012; Jackson, 2013). The overall length of the retrospective PhD by publication is often shorter because the research has already been completed.

While misguidedly regarded by some as an 'easy option', a PhD by publication is not without its challenges (Lee et al., 2012; Peacock, 2017). Co-authors are usually required to provide written confirmation of the student's involvement in the production of a paper (Rees et al., 2019). There can be considerable variations between institutions and also internationally in the requirements of a PhD by publication. These differences can include:

- The number and type of papers required
- The type of publication in which the paper(s) should be published
- The nature and extent of the student's contribution to the papers
- Whether supervisors should be included in authorship
- The way in which the papers are drawn together in the thesis.

(Mullins and Kiley, 2002; Lee et al., 2012; Jackson, 2013)

If you are considering undertaking this type of doctorate, it is essential that you establish the exact requirements of the institution. Another challenge to consider is the fact that securing publication in peer-review journals is becoming more challenging, particularly in the period immediately prior to a REF. Covering the cost of open access publications, which is particularly desired by some disciplines, can also be problematic. In addition, the student must deal with the potential rejection of papers and therefore having to submit their paper(s) to subsequent journals. Making required changes to papers in the light of reviewer feedback can be a lengthy process and long delays may be experienced awaiting final editorial decisions (Lee et al., 2012; Jackson, 2013).

Case study 3.7

As part of his senior academic role, Rex has been seconded to work part-time on a number of research projects over recent years. These projects have culminated in a number of peer-reviewed publications in international journals. Rex's time working on these studies and publications prevented him from starting a doctorate and he began to become anxious that he was being 'left behind' by his colleagues. He therefore commenced a PhD by publication. Working on the accompanying 'narrative' was much more challenging than he had anticipated. He also encountered difficulty in securing the publication of the final paper which tied his body of work together. Nevertheless, Rex still felt he made the right choice of doctorate.

Which type of doctorate should I undertake?

Assuming that you are an academic who will be undertaking a part-time doctorate at your home institution, the answer to the question 'Which type of doctorate should I do?' is the same as that for all potential doctoral students ... you should do the one that is right for you. However, you should clarify the requirements of your home institution regarding the particular doctoral route that you are considering. You should also clarify the doctoral programme requirements of any other institutions that you are considering, because they could be different from those of your home institution. Do not make any assumptions. Thinking about how the structure of the doctorate will sit alongside your preferred style of working and learning and your workload is also important. This is the time to clarify your institution's policies on designated study time and sabbaticals so that you can map these and plan ahead.

It can be difficult not to be swayed by the decisions that your friends and colleagues have made or the preference of your line manager or home institution. Nevertheless, whatever you decide should ultimately be *your* choice. Your decision must be right for you. It is important that you weigh up the pros and cons of the different options available. You should consider what would be the right doctorate for you now and over the coming years. As we will see in later chapters, moments of self-doubt are unfortunately common for most students at some point during a doctorate. However, if you start a doctorate feeling uncomfortable or pressurised about the choices that you have made, your overall experience is likely to be that much more challenging. The following reflective activity should help you to finalise your decisions. It is crucial that you are honest about yourself.

Reflection 3.1

Reflect on your *strengths*, *limitations* and *needs* in relation to:

- Undertaking a doctorate in your home institution
- Undertaking a doctorate in an external institution
- Selecting from the different types of doctorate available to you

In the following chapter we will explore the transferable skills that academics may already have which will facilitate their doctoral progression. We also consider the skills development that academics may require.

To access the online resources accompanying this chapter, please visit:
https://study.sagepub.com/harvey

Four

Transitioning to the doctorate experience

Transferable skills training and personal development are integral to postgraduate studying. Therefore, postgraduate research students are required to regularly take stock of the skills they already possess and those they need to develop when reviewing the progress of their doctoral journey. However, as we already know, in most universities the doctorate is designed around the needs of the traditional three-year full-time student, and even when provision is made for those who are part-time students, it is far less likely to take into account the development needs of those already working full-time in academia.

This group of postgraduate research students are often juggling with their own teaching commitments and so have little time to prioritise their own personal development, instead giving precedence to that which is necessary for their teaching roles. Often the expectation is that due to their positions and the duties they carry out, they will already have developed sufficient transferable skills to enable them to successfully navigate their doctorate. While this is true to some extent, as skills such as personal leadership, team working, project management and communicating complex ideas to different audiences are most likely to have been honed during their academic careers, other skills important for doctoral study may not have been developed. The assumption, then, that postgraduate research students who are academics have the know-how, resilience and motivation to cope is one that should be dispelled. Akin to other postgraduate research students, those working full-time in academia are likely to have a number of personal development needs that they will need to address. They are likely to need some guidance and support from their supervisors as to how to best address any skill deficits they may have. However, they may feel anxious and find it embarrassing or difficult to ask for help, and fear that admitting to any kind of development need could be a slur on their own academic integrity.

This chapter hopes to dispel any misconceptions about personal development planning and its significance for all postgraduate research students, including those working in academia. It is absolutely essential to start with the end in sight, so you do not lose track of where you are heading. We firmly believe that personal development planning can greatly assist you in the six to eight years it takes to complete a part-time doctorate, so that you are able to meet your submission deadline. Although many readers will be used to the personal development process, as it is likely to form part of your annual performance review, personal development during the doctoral journey has a different purpose. Personal development planning in this context is fundamentally concerned with your progress as a postgraduate research student rather than your full-time employment, and discussions and actions must reflect this.

This chapter begins by setting out the case for taking a personal development approach for the doctoral journey. It includes the importance of identifying and valuing the skills you already have as a postgraduate research student as well as seeking ways to address any gaps in your skill-set. It offers guidance on how to create a personal development plan, including the monitoring and evaluation of the postgraduate research student's progress, and it introduces the concept of reflection in the context of doctoral studies. It discusses how using approaches such as journaling can be extremely helpful. We hope that in reading this chapter, and working through the activities presented, you will have a clearer idea of your own development needs and that you will feel comfortable and confident about how you can identify, address and record your progress and achievements.

The need for a personal development approach

The issue of transferable skills is not likely to quicken the pulse of most postgraduate research students, especially those who already have an established career in academia and have developed a high level of skills that could be transferable to doctoral-level study. In fact, focusing on your personal development could be seen to be a distraction from getting on with the 'research' itself. Let's face it, in the busy world of academia with the ever-increasing piles of marking, teaching, tutorials and the myriad of other tasks required by lecturing staff, who seriously has time to think about their own personal development? After all, surely that's what the doctorate is about, isn't it? Well, yes and no. It is true that during your doctoral studies you will, by necessity, develop a skill-set that you did not have before. However, in order to broaden your abilities, on the road to becoming an effective researcher and successfully completing your doctoral degree, it would be wise to put aside a period of time to think about the skills you already possess and those that you may need to develop. This is important for, as the saying goes, 'those who fail to plan, plan to fail'. We think this is true in relation to acquiring the skills required of a doctoral researcher, some of which you may have long been concerned about, as well as others that you have recently come to recognise as being important.

Reflection 4.1

Spend some time reflecting on your previous educational experiences including any continuing personal development, either formal or informal.

Which skills did you excel in and how did you know this?

Which, if any, areas did you find challenging and how did you address them?

Why do you need a personal development plan?

It is widely accepted that people learn in different ways and have different needs. Taking a personal development approach recognises this and can help you to become aware of your own personal preferences, in terms of your learning, as well as helping you to identify your strengths. It may help you to consider personal development planning using the analogy set out in the reflective exercise below.

Reflection 4.2

Have you ever set out on an intentional trip without planning where you would stay and what you would do while you were there?
Take a few moments to imagine that you did and what that may have looked and felt like.

We would imagine that almost certainly you would become anxious and frustrated. Your thoughts would continuously be focused on trying to plan everything during the journey instead of enjoying the actual experience of travelling to your destination. We think it would be very difficult to be able to enjoy the trip if you were frantically trying to book suitable accommodation and to work out just what you would do during your stay. It would be so much easier if this had been taken care of before starting your journey, as you would have given some thought to the places you wished to visit and the things you wanted to do. I am sure we would all agree that it would be so much easier if you had some sort of plan. This applies equally to your doctoral journey. With little or no planning, postgraduate researchers can end up frustrated and disheartened when they fail to make the progress they hoped for. Not having a plan could result in time and energy being wasted. This is something that most part-time postgraduate researchers are desperate to avoid, as time pressure is such a challenge for them. In working with doctoral students, we have come to recognise that some people get a buzz or adrenaline rush from 'winging' it or 'flying by the seat of their pants', yet this rarely leads to success for such substantive work as that required for a doctorate, as illustrated by Davina's experiences.

Case study 4.1

Davina has a long-established career in academia. The focus of her research is an area she is passionate about and has spent the vast majority of her career working in. Some years into her doctoral research, problems emerged which revealed a complete lack of planning in relation to her study. Davina had little idea of the most appropriate approach for her study and had muddled on in spite of the pleas by her supervisor to meet up to discuss her plans. She often allowed weeks to pass by without engaging in her research. This was followed by a hectic period of collecting a copious amount of data without a clear vision of where she was heading and the desired outcomes for the research. Her problems were compounded when her supervisor suddenly left the institution in which Davina was registered. It took time to find a replacement supervisor, who did their best to try to help. However, following an unsuccessful viva, which had to be convened because Davina's period of registration was expiring, she quit her doctoral studies. She states that the problems were insurmountable and the impact on her health and well-being was just too much to even think about trying to complete her doctorate.

Thankfully, these types of scenario are rare. The progression of students is far more tightly monitored nowadays, with safeguards such as progression panels being an inherent part of the journey, as explained in Chapter 5. However, in Davina's case, it would appear that these safeguards were either not in place or the guidance given was not heeded, leading to an undesirable outcome. We can't help but think that things may have been very different if she had spent time working out her development plan, as this would have given her a focus and may have prevented the downward spiral in which she seems to have become trapped. Sprints and stops are to be expected during your journey. However, a good plan will help you to plot a path towards your desired outcome of achieving your doctorate within the designated timeframe. A well-thought-out personal development plan will facilitate you in making considered decisions and help to prevent you stagnating, going around in circles or moving backwards. It will also help you to get back on track when things do not go according to plan. A personal development plan is beneficial for your emotional health and well-being, as having a sense of purposefulness, of knowing what you are aiming for and how you will get there can minimise stress and anxiety, even when there are hiccups.

The vast majority of universities, certainly in the United Kingdom but internationally as well, including growing numbers of those in the United States and Australia, now include as part of the offering to postgraduate research study the opportunity to access training programmes and developmental opportunities across a wide range of skills. These may include training in managing the anxieties of a doctorate, critical thinking, research methodology, academic writing, literacy and information searching skills, networking and conference presentations, and may be complimented by specific training at a faculty or department level. These are skills that are rarely discussed in an annual performance review where you are likely to be considering personal development in terms of your teaching role. It is crucial that you make good use of the training opportunities that are appropriate for you, especially in those areas of training that are not mandatory but which may be important in addressing the specific skills that you need to have. Do consider also revisiting skills that you think you already possess. Doing so can prove to be a useful refresher at the very least and you may even learn something new. Your personal development plan should reflect these issues and the time you need to attend to developing your skills.

Your personal development plan is something that you should discuss and agree with your supervisory team early on in your studies. Your supervisors should be keen to work with you to ensure that your development needs are identified and addressed in a timely fashion. This is essential in order for you to progress as effectively as you can with your studies. However, dependent on who your supervisors are, and their perception of with whom responsibility for this area of your doctorate lies, you may have to initiate conversations about your development needs yourself. Your supervisors may believe that as someone employed within academia, you should be attuned to identifying and responding to your own development requirements and therefore not feel the need to talk to you about this area of your studies. They may believe that raising such issues is a little paternalistic and so avoid the topic altogether. This may be especially true if your supervisors are junior to you in terms of professional status or if they are younger than you are. Or they may see this aspect of the research degree trajectory as not their business, and instead point you in the direction of any available in-house seminars or workshops, leaving you to navigate your own way through.

Thankfully, there are some very useful resources to help, as your development as a researcher should not be left to chance. Many universities, at least in the UK, are now aligned to a personal and professional development framework, such as the VITAE Researcher Development Framework, which was launched in 2010 (VITAE, 2010a). If you have read Chapter 3, you may remember being introduced to the VITAE website, where this framework is housed (www.vitae.ac.uk/). The link is also included on the online resources for this chapter. This industry standard framework has been developed in partnership with a number of stakeholders, including researchers, funders and employers, with the aim of helping postgraduate degree research students, including those already established in their academic careers, during and beyond their doctoral journey. It is a statement of the knowledge, skills and behaviours that characterise an effective and skilled researcher. It covers four domains:

- Knowledge and intellectual abilities
- Personal effectiveness
- Research governance and organisation
- Engagement, influence and impact.

Most doctoral training programmes, at least those in British universities, but also increasingly further afield, will be designed around these domains.

The Researcher Development Framework (VITAE, 2010a) is available as a professional development planner that is downloadable and so is easily accessible. The weblink for accessing the framework is available on the book's online resources. The framework can help you to identify the specific areas that you wish to develop further. It is also useful for generating an action plan that will help you to achieve your goals.

Every postgraduate research student will have a different personal development plan and therefore a different action plan. Your plan should therefore reflect your skills needs over the period of your research degree as well as any longer-term personal and professional development goals that you have. Going forward, it may even help to inform your annual performance review, although it is important to acknowledge that there will be fundamental differences in the aims of these two development plans.

We would suggest that your initial personal development plan focuses on the period up to the probation review, which is usually at the end of the second year for part-time students. It is wise, however, to check when exactly this is likely to be with your particular institution, what the process involves, and do keep a note of this very important date so that you are well prepared for it. Following on from your probation review, you will be in a position to develop and agree an updated development and action plan for the reminder of your doctoral journey.

We would argue that postgraduate research students who are also already established in an academic career will find the Researcher Development Framework (VITAE, 2010a) just as useful as full-time or other part-time doctoral students, as it will provide you with a comprehensive, recognised format for identifying and communicating your development needs as well as your skills. This could prove to be invaluable when funding decisions are being made in terms of training and it is also a useful record of your capabilities when discussing any potential promotion opportunities in the future.

Whatever your experience or background, developing your training plan as outlined above is important, as many academic staff who are studying for a doctorate part-time enter academia with professional backgrounds and a skill-set that is not closely aligned to those of a researcher. In your professional life you may have relied on learning knowledge and the accepted ways of doing things. Having a good knowledge base and the skill to recall it accurately are important. However, doctoral work will require you to move beyond this, to take advantage of new opportunities, to problematise accepted discourse, to speculate, explore, experiment and innovate. Personal development planning can equip you with the skills to do this so that you can engage, with confidence, in the higher-level cognitive skills required to generate ideas, create and analyse concepts, synthesise ideas and design solutions to problems. Remember that acquiring such skills is an investment in your research journey and is an important aspect of your doctoral studies, so it is well worth investing in them. However, before you are in a position to address your development needs, you need to know what they are and this will require you to carry out some self-assessment as you may well identify strengths you did not recognise you had and needs that you had not considered previously and so were unaware that these were areas for development.

The first stage of this process is a self-evaluation of your current skills and strengths. This type of self-evaluation may be a formal process, facilitated by your university, which is included as part of the induction programme and supported by meetings with your supervisors. However, as we have discussed, there is no guarantee that this will be the case and you may find that you need to carry out this activity by yourself. The VITAE (VITAE, 2010b) web-based Researcher Development Framework Planner can help you with this process. As we have outlined, it is an incredibly useful resource and will prove indispensable for those who are not naturally reflective, which is a key aspect of analysing and evaluating your learning needs. You will need to register with VITAE to access this resource. Note that registration is free to all doctoral students and academics. The activity below will be a good investment of your time at this stage.

Activity 4.1

Complete the personal development needs analysis found on the book's online resources. Once completed, you can map this to the VITAE Researcher Development Framework Planner (VITAE, 2010b).

Remember to share this with your supervisors so that you can discuss your needs and any concerns as well as your progress in addressing them.

You will need to be honest in owning up to your development needs and not see this as losing professional face or a slur on your identity as an academic. We know that this is especially difficult for those doctoral students who have many years' experience of working in academia and who are seen as the experts in their own field. However, unless you have already achieved a doctorate, you will not have had the opportunity to develop all the skills needed for this intellectually and emotionally challenging journey. You therefore owe it to yourself to access the development and training that you need to be successful. There may be others within your own institution or networks who also need the specific training that you have identified for yourself, and you may be able to collaborate with them to ensure that this training need is met. The good news is that as an academic you will most likely already possess many of the skills required and it is just as important to acknowledge these.

The development needs that we have identified during our own studies or have been raised by doctoral students whom we know include:

- Developing literacy and information searching skills
- Improving academic writing and critical analysis skills
- Acquiring advanced information technology skills
- Acquiring research governance approval
- Writing documents for participants, such as information sheets and consent forms
- Document management
- Applying for funding, for example, for travel costs to attend a conference or a workshop
- Drafting abstracts and manuscripts for conferences and journals
- Attending conferences and networking with other researchers
- Collaborating with researchers from other disciplines or institutions
- Producing a research poster or giving a research presentation
- Exploring opportunities for disseminating and/or commercialising their research.

There is no need to worry if you have identified lots of different development needs. Instead, see these as opportunities to acquire new and exciting skills. As we all learn in different ways, look out for activities that will help you to address your identified needs in a way that will work for you. If this does not exist in the institution in which you are studying, it may be an opportunity for the doctorate school or similar department to develop a workshop or another learning activity to address this gap. Your supervisor may be able to help you with this. If nothing is available in-house, then seek out any online or virtual learning environment resources, seminars or workshops that may be available within your own or another institution. Remember that these things vary across faculties, schools and departments, so do check what is happening elsewhere within your own institution. Budgets for personal development may be seen to be the remit of full-time postgraduates, but remember the old adage, 'if you don't ask, you won't get'. If funding is not available from the doctoral budget, your line manager may be able to help. Always check, therefore, if there is any funding you can access which will help towards the cost of meeting any development needs that you have identified but which you cannot access free of charge. Blogs have become an increasingly popular way of communicating and finding out just what is available. Postgraduate research students from the University of Manchester highlight a number of blogs frequented and populated by doctoral students and they are well worth investigating these (see the link below). You may find something, as they say, 'to make you laugh, inspire or motivate you'.

How to achieve your goals

Activity 4.2

Revisit your personal development needs analysis. Select between five and ten goals which are important for you to achieve and arrange them in the order in which you will address them.

As we have already identified, setting specific goals is something you should do as early on in your studies as possible. In order for you to effectively plan and manage your work and achieve your goals, bearing in mind the other commitments you are likely to have, it is important that all of your goals are SMART. They should therefore be:

Specific – Exactly what is it you want to achieve?

Measurable – How will you know you have achieved it?

Agreed – Do your supervisors agree with your goals?

Realistic – Can your objectives be achieved given the time and resources available to you?

Timed – When do you expect to have met each goal?

(Adapted from Cottrell, 2019)

At the beginning of your doctorate, and as already suggested, you may find it easier to develop two separate but related sets of goals. The first of these are the detailed goals leading up to the probation review. The second set of goals should cover the remainder of the doctorate and include both the research element and the writing-up stage that you will need to undertake to complete and submit your thesis on time. As you define your goals, we would suggest that you:

- Start with the date by which you will need to complete your probation review or submit your thesis.
- Consider carefully each individual activity or task that you will need to complete and the order in which you will tackle them.
- If your institution has a process whereby a draft of your thesis is submitted for critical review, allow plenty of time for this to happen. It is also crucial that you allow sufficient time for your supervisors to read and comment on your thesis before you submit it for examination, as you will need to consider and respond to any suggested corrections. A realistic amount of time is an absolute minimum of three months, but it may be considerably longer depending on your own and your supervisor's other commitments.
- Do allow some flexibility in your schedule in case things don't quite go according to plan. It is also important to schedule in time for breaks and any commitments related to your employment.

Setting and achieving goals has been brought into sharp focus recently as the Covid-19 outbreak has meant that many teaching staff have found themselves in the position of having to reschedule teaching as well as preparing online delivery and additional resources – something which could not have been anticipated. It has been a very time-intensive period for all concerned, and has resulted in many doctoral students with teaching responsibilities being forced to put aside their studies in order to focus on meeting the demands so suddenly placed on them. Although it is very unlikely that whatever does crop up will have anything near the impact as the current pandemic, when the unexpected does happen, a little slack in the schedule can go a long way in helping you to deal with the unanticipated.

Once you have defined your goals, you will need to think about how you wish to present them. It is usual to do this in the form of a Gannt chart (you can find free Gantt chart templates on the online resources), although some people like to use a different format, such as a list or a table. However, presenting your goals in a Gannt chart has the advantage of making them clearly visible and therefore easier for both you and your supervisors to see where you are at any point in time. Gannt charts can help in keeping you on track and showing you where there has been any slippage that may impact on your completion time.

It is important that both your skills development and your goals are shared, discussed and agreed with your supervisors as they are in a prime position to provide valuable advice on whether your goals are appropriate and realistic. If you are off course, they should be able to help you to get back on track. It would be prudent to give careful thought to their suggestions and advice. This does not mean that you have to agree with everything they say, of course, but do consider and discuss with them anything that you are not happy about, rather than letting it fester.

An important point to note here is that transitioning to being a part-time doctoral student requires a balancing of roles which can be difficult to manage and may be a challenge to your professional identity as you shift to a position of student while maintaining your role as expert in your own field. Many people cope with this transition with few, if any, problems, but others can find it a bit tricky to navigate. So it is as well to give this issue some thought and talk it over, if necessary, with someone you trust.

Reflection 4.3

Reflect on your thoughts about transitioning from the role of expert in your field to that of a novice postgraduate researcher.

What five things are you looking forward to?

What things do you think may be a challenge?

What will you do to address your own feelings about your new position?

Who can you speak to about this?

The difference in your identity is something that many postgraduate research students with accomplished careers struggle with. Having a personal development plan can reap dividends in helping you to identify any development needs and how you will meet them, so that you are able to keep on track. It can seem like a difficult path to navigate, as though you are in a liminal space of betwixt and between, as you are both expert and novice, with a foot in both camps, so to speak. However, there are a myriad of positives that it is certainly worth reflecting on.

One of the most attractive of these is that being a postgraduate research student gives you the freedom, to a large extent, to set your own path and the opportunity to examine in-depth an aspect of your discipline that you find fascinating. However, the other side of the coin is that if things do go wrong, it is down to you to deal with them. Your supervisors will do what they can to help, but progression and successful completion of your doctorate is essentially your responsibility. The supervisor's role is to be facilitative rather than controlling. It is therefore down to you to plan how you will reach your end point. Do remember the case study of Davina, who failed to plan and, in effect, planned her own demise. As we have discussed, being proactive in how you will progress through your studies means identifying, analysing and actioning your personal and professional development needs so that you can meet your goals. Be aware that although you will have a schedule for your doctorate, with a chronological sequence of steps that you will need to work through, in reality you are likely to find that you will go through many stages of revising and replacing work you have already completed. Do also remember that your goals are not set in stone, and that you will need to monitor and review them during the course of your studies. This will help you to keep abreast of your progress and check if anything needs to be changed, so that you can complete your doctorate on time.

If you find yourself in a position where you are concerned that things are getting difficult, it is important to find someone to speak to about it. If you have not already done so, complete Activity 4.1 and Reflection 4.3. It can be very helpful and a boost to your confidence and self-esteem to know that others have felt exactly the same and have come through to the other end. It is hard to remember this when you are feeling very anxious, stressed or frustrated. At the very least, do visit the book's online resouces, which contain a number of links to helpful websites and blogs. These can be a real source of support and inspiration when you are feeling lost or low and have forgotten that everybody goes through these phases. It's easy to compare studying for a doctorate to your normal 'day job', but you need to recall that the things you are already practised in will be much easier for you to do than the things which are new and somewhat unknown to you. To compare studying for a doctorate to the practice that you are well versed in means that you are likely setting yourself up to experience feelings of inadequacy and demotivation.

We think this is also true for those undertaking a professional doctorate, such as a Doctor of Education (EdD) or Doctor of Business Administration (DBA). Just as with the more traditional PhD, these doctorates require evidence of a rigorous approach to research as well as a contribution to an element of new knowledge. These are skills that you will need to demonstrate and evidence, using advanced skills of analysis and synthesis. Such higher-level skills are outlined by Anderson et al. (2001), who present a revised version of Bloom's Taxonomy (originally published in 1956). The taxonomy is a logical universal framework which was designed to help educators and researchers to understand the principal ways in which individuals acquire and develop new knowledge, skills and understandings. However, as Miller (1957) cites, our mental capacity to remember and work with lots of information simultaneously is limited. Therefore, we would suggest that you break any large tasks down into between five and nine elements or sub-goals and tackle each in turn, in order to meet your overall goal. Bearing in mind that you will most likely be working at a level higher than that to which you are accustomed, working in this way will help you to manage your schedule, identify any risks and adjust your plan accordingly.

Doctoral degrees are by definition flexible and dynamic. The journey may take you along a path that you had not anticipated, and so it is important to be adaptable to change rather than sticking rigorously to a framework that you developed in the past but is no longer working for you. For this reason, we would suggest that as you progress with your studies, you revisit your goals often and try to improve on them. The trick here is to set yourself goals that are reasonable, and a little challenging, but not so demanding that you are in a constant state of anxiety in trying to meet them. When reviewing your goals, try to find someone – maybe a peer or a colleague who has recently completed their own doctorate or perhaps with peers during a doctoral forum or other such meeting – to assist you in exploring your goals. You could ask them to really press you to explore and discuss your development needs and goals and how you have gone about meeting them. Ask them about their own goals and interests too. It can be helpful in motivating you and in generating ideas for tackling any goals that you are still striving towards. Exploring your goals with a colleague can therefore be useful in a number of ways:

- They can bring a fresh pair of eyes to a situation
- They can take an objective stance
- They can ask the questions you won't ask yourself and so stimulate deeper reflection
- They may offer different perspectives on events
- They may validate your thoughts
- They may contribute to your understanding from a different knowledge and skills base
- They may suggest alternative sources of action.

The Society for Research into Higher Education (SRHE) is an organisation that seeks to promote research into all aspects of higher education. We would argue that it is especially useful for postgraduate research students, as it runs conferences and development seminars on a range of topics, such as different methodological approaches, conference presentations and writing for publication. It also organises a number of specialist network groups, some of which may be of interest to you. Do visit their website (https://www.srhe.ac.uk/).

Recording your personal development

Personal development requires you not only to make a plan, discuss and then follow it, but to recognise, as we have considered above, that it is a process which is individual to each person and that they will shape their plan to suit their own needs and interests over time. A reflective process is a good way of monitoring your personal progress, as being reflective encourages deep self-awareness. The problem with busy academics, especially those taking on the additional task of a doctorate, is that reflection is often an early casualty when there is time pressure. If this is true for you, this may be a good time to remind yourself of the benefits of taking a reflective approach.

As outlined by Jasper (2006), these include:

- Achieving a purpose
- Ordering your thoughts
- Creating a permanent record
- Being creative
- Developing your analytical skills
- Developing your critical thinking skills
- Developing new understandings and knowledge
- Demonstrating that you understand something.

Whether or not you use a structured reflective framework is your decision entirely, but Jasper (2006) provides a critical review of those frameworks most commonly used. However, we would argue that the skills listed above are endemic to doctoral-level study, and that recording your reflections in writing is useful in facilitating your development and progress and in evaluating your goals. Writing as a form of reflection involves you committing your thoughts and ideas into words. It is useful because writing something down that you may have been musing about for some time means that those thoughts become externalised and open to your own scrutiny, as well as those of others if you choose to share them.

Reflection 4.4

How will recording your reflections help you?
   We think that recording your reflections in this way can aid you in thinking further about areas that you have been contemplating and therefore promote deeper understanding. Once your thoughts are put into words and written down, they are captured, meaning that you can revisit them at any point in the future.

Bryan's case study illustrates how he made good use of reflection as he conducted his doctoral research. His reflection below illustrates well the importance of putting ideas into words.

Case study 4.2

It made sense for me to map how I was doing with my research. I remember writing about some of the difficulties I was having trying to present my data in writing up my thesis. Writing is an obvious way for me to keep track of what's going on – in many ways it's easier than trying to talk about it. It really helped with my anxieties at that time and helped me to put things into perspective. (Bryan)

Some postgraduate research students, especially those with a background in social science, education or the helping professions, may find writing about their ideas easier than others, as reflecting on their practice and progress is likely to have been part of their prior learning experience. For others, the concept of writing reflectively may be new and something they are not at all sure about. They may be more used to processing events and experiences in their heads. However, it can be easy to forget things that may seem important at the time, if they are not recorded in some way. We would suggest that recording how your skills are developing and what you find challenging in some sort of journal is crucial to your personal development as a postgraduate research student. An additional benefit is that it gives you a basis for your discussion at your supervision meetings and can be a good way of starting these meetings, helping you to remember important issues that you would like to discuss. If you are not naturally reflective and are unsure of how to start your reflective journal, you could adopt the approach suggested by Rainer (1978), who is a guru in the journal writing literature. You could begin by completing sentences such as:

- I know …
- I want …
- I think …
- I remember …
- I wish ….
- I wonder if …
- I'm worried about …

Another way to start your reflective writing is to write a list. This works well for people who are very hesitant to the idea of keeping a reflective journal, but may have been requested to do so by their supervisors. You could begin with a topic such as:

- Something that you have been spending a lot of time thinking about and may be keeping you awake at night
- Things you want to discuss in your next supervision meeting
- Five things that have gone well
- Five things that are proving to be challenging at the moment
- Immediate events and experiences

Moving on from writing a list or completing sentences can lead to change. Perhaps there is something that you just want to clarify your thinking about. Writing, reading and adding to or altering your reflective writing may help you to clear your mind. As one postgraduate research student reported:

> … reflection is a habit that everyone can learn. I can really understand that now. I would put it like this: it makes a difference, between fifteen years of experience or only one year of experience repeated 15 times, … it works for me.

The following is a list of tips, based on our own experiences, as well as those of colleagues and students we have worked with:

- Choose a safe place to begin your reflective journaling, where you will not be disturbed and you can feel relaxed.
- Choose a way of expressing yourself that is easiest for you, including doodling or drawing.
- Try not to worry about spellings, punctuations or grammar; school rules don't apply in this type of writing.
- Remember that no one but you will see this writing, unless you choose to share it with them of course.
- Remember to safeguard your writing, so that you, and you alone, can control who can access it. Use a password-protected file or, if handwriting your journal, make sure you keep your notebook safe, so that you don't lose it.

You may wish at this stage to read a reflective blog by Michelle Beattie, a lecturer, who completed a part-time PhD at the University of Stirling. Her blog sets out the benefits of reflective journaling as she grappled with her feelings of insecurity during her studies. You will find the internet address on the book's online resources.

We believe that journaling in this way can be an incredibly effective way of documenting your progress towards your goals, and your thoughts and feelings as you are working towards achieving them. Writing about your progress and achievements can be hugely satisfying and a real motivator for times when you are feeling low or when things are not going quite to plan. Reflective journaling can also help you to work through difficult situations, to find your own solutions to problems and to bring clarity when things feel muddled. There can also be benefits to your emotional health and well-being, as writing reflectively about the difficult situations that you are facing can help you to examine things from a range of perspectives and reduce anxiety. Writing a reflective journal can also be a useful precursor to writing up your thesis. You will already have started to document your progress and can use your experience of journal writing to help you to cope with the stress that is intrinsic to this intense period of the doctoral journey.

To summarise, this chapter has focused on the transition from employee to part-time postgraduate research student and has highlighted both the positives as well as the challenges that are endemic to this transition. We have discussed how taking a personal development approach can be helpful in navigating the doctoral journey and have argued that to be successful in your research degree you will need from the very start to have:

- A clear idea of what you want to do and how you are going to do it
- An honest approach to reflecting on and reporting your progress
- A determination to get things done and manage any problems that might arise.

We also discussed the importance of carrying out a self-assessment of your development needs and explained how this will help you to:

- Record your skills, strengths and development needs
- Formulate a plan for your development which takes into account your current work and other commitments
- Implement your plan, making good use of any resources that may be accessible to you at your institution and wider afield.

Finally, we have discussed the benefits of taking a reflective approach to recording your personal and professional development, outlining how this can help you to:

- Clarify muddled or unclear thinking
- Identify and solve problems
- Minimise anxiety and frustration when things are not going to plan
- Get you back on track
- Act as a springboard for discussion in meetings with your supervisor.

To access the online resources accompanying this chapter, please visit:
https://study.sagepub.com/harvey

Five

Supervision during your doctoral journey

The relationship between a doctoral student and their supervisor or supervisory team is a crucial one. It is therefore essential that you consider how you will develop and maintain a positive relationship with your supervisory team right from the beginning of your doctoral journey. All doctoral students would be wise to reflect on how they will work with their supervisors to ensure a doctoral journey that is as uneventful as possible and that culminates in a successful outcome. However, for those doctoral students already working in academia there are additional factors regarding supervision that may come into play.

This chapter provides an overview of the key issues that we consider to be paramount in enabling you to develop and maintain a positive relationship with your supervisory team. This relationship should be based on mutual trust and understanding. It should support you in reaching your end goal of the successful and timely completion of your doctorate. Issues considered within this chapter include: the allocation of supervisors; how to start the relationship; strategies for best managing the student–supervisor relationship; the benefits and limitations of being supervised by someone you already have a working relationship with; and what to do if problems arise. We hope that engaging with this chapter will help you to develop a way of working with your supervisory team which is supportive and facilitative, in which roles and responsibilities are clearly defined. For clarity, we refer throughout this chapter to your 'supervisory team', although we acknowledge that some doctoral students will have just one supervisor (see below).

Allocation of the supervisor

Once accepted onto a doctoral programme your progression and the doctoral processes and procedures will be overseen by the institution's doctoral college (or similarly-named organisation). A critical matter to be quickly established is the allocation of your supervisory team and the doctoral college will usually take the lead in this process. For any doctoral student, the relationship with their supervisory team will be a key factor during their programme of study. You may have experience of the supervisee–supervisor relationship in the context of your own student caseload. However, the doctoral student–supervisor relationship can be substantially different. The potential impact of the academic level of doctoral study and the extended time involved (noting that it is usually twice the length for part-time students) should not be underestimated. The possible additional complexities of the student–supervisor relationship between those who already know each other, or who in other contexts work alongside each other, can compound the situation. While this can have its benefits, there is also the potential to generate a conflict of interest for those involved during the doctorate.

How many supervisors do I need?

The institution's regulations will determine the number of supervisors allocated to a doctoral student. The usual number is two, with at least one being from that institution. However, many doctorates have been successfully completed with one supervisor. Conversely, some students will have three supervisors, particularly if two have limited supervisory experience. The third, more experienced, supervisor usually takes on a more distant role, which is primarily to mentor the less experienced supervisors. In some institutions, the number of supervisors may be determined by the availability of those meeting the institution's criteria and those with subject specialism or research method knowledge. In some cases, a subject expert will be part of the team in a more advisory, rather than supervisory, capacity. We advocate that students undertaking a doctorate in their home institution should have at least two supervisors. This should reduce the likelihood of conflicts of interest, which we will discuss later in this chapter. When there are two or more supervisors, one will usually take the leading role (sometimes referred to as the 'Director of Studies' or 'Lead Supervisor'). They will have ultimate responsibility for ensuring the required academic and doctoral procedures are followed. This includes the submission of progression assessment documentation.

Case study 5.1

Cora had just one supervisor during her doctorate. She was not aware at the start of her studies that this was unusual. It was only when she talked to colleagues undertaking their doctorate at other institutions that she became aware that her situation was different. However, she was unconcerned about this. Cora felt that she had a good relationship with her supervisor and that she benefited from a consistent approach to her supervision. The doctoral college at the institution had a strong presence and Cora felt that she was aware of individuals she could approach if difficulties with her supervisor arose.

Allocation of your supervisory team

Some institutions involve the student in deciding who their supervisor(s) will be. In other cases, students will be allocated supervisors as a *fait accompli*. Most commonly, supervisors will be in-house to the institution where the doctorate is undertaken. While a supervisor who is based at an external institution can bring a different perspective and specialist knowledge or experience, arranging supervisory meetings can be more challenging. In addition, increasing financial restrictions may mean that an institution will want to keep supervisory teams in-house as much as possible. Proceeding to appoint an external supervisor may therefore require clear justification before it is approved.

If you are undertaking your doctorate at your home institution, it is very likely that you will know and perhaps have worked alongside at least one of your supervisors before you set out on your doctorate. Furthermore, your supervisor could be your line manager, a close friend or you might be their line manager. This is not necessarily problematic if all parties are comfortable with this arrangement and feel that they would be able to keep the differing aspects of their role separate. Indeed, there are potential benefits for some students working alongside a supervisor who already knows and understands them. However, all parties involved should at least consider the potential impact in both the short and longer term of a prior or ongoing working relationship and/or friendship. We suggest that for most students and supervisors this situation is best avoided, especially where a friendship is already established or where line management is a factor.

A student would be naive to request supervision from a friend in the hope that they will be overly kind or lenient. Conversely, the supervisory–student relationship in this situation could be seriously compromised, in addition to any longer-term working relationships or friendships. Nevertheless, this may be unavoidable if supervisor availability is limited, or where specific subject or research methodology knowledge is required. It is important that you do not 'pin your hopes' on being allocated your choice of supervisor(s). There are many factors that your doctoral college will need to take into consideration, some of which you will not necessarily be aware of. You do not want to set yourself up for a major disappointment. In saying this, if there is an individual who has particular expertise in your subject area or methodology, there is no harm in making this known to the doctoral research college and expressing a preference. However, as discussed, be aware that there should be no expectation that you will be allocated your preferred supervisor. Conversely, if there is a potential supervisor who you know with absolute certainty that you would be unable to work with (for whatever reason), it would be prudent to raise this in a professional manner with the doctoral college. This should be done at the earliest opportunity before the allocation of your supervisors has been finalised.

All doctoral students, wherever they are studying, should feel comfortable with their supervisory team, whoever they are. Once your doctorate has begun, if you feel there is a good reason why the relationship might be compromised, then you should alert the doctoral college. The institution should have a mechanism in place to change the configuration of a supervisory team without creating additional tension to the parties involved. If you feel strongly that an allocated supervisor would not be the right person for you, then do not wait to see how things pan out, only to have to pursue reallocation later on. It makes sense to communicate your concerns with the doctoral college as early as possible. It is often easier all round to make a change to the proposed supervisory team early, rather than later on when supervisory teams for all newly enrolled students have been finalised. It may be more difficult to find someone who has capacity to take on a new student part-way through a doctorate or someone who will balance the knowledge and experience of the supervisory team.

Do remember, however, that you must have a good reason for requesting a change to your supervisory team. Anecdotal claims that supervisors are strict with students are not likely to be accepted as valid reasons. Sometimes unanticipated problems arise later on. Situations when student–supervisor relationships are compromised or break down are discussed later in this chapter.

Whether you are undertaking your doctorate at your home or an external institution, it is always best to 'be prepared' with regard to the allocation of your supervisory team. The following activity will help you to ensure you are suitably informed and equipped.

Activity 5.1

If you will be undertaking your doctorate in your home institution, find out what involvement you are likely to have in determining the configuration of your supervisory team.

If you will be undertaking your doctorate in your home institution, identify who could potentially be part of your supervisory team (regardless of whether you will have a say in the allocation). Identify the benefits and potential challenges to all parties involved of their being part of your supervisory team.

If you are planning to undertake your doctorate at an external institution, access listings of research/academic staff to ascertain who your potential supervisor(s) might be. Identify the benefits and potential challenges to you of their being part of your supervisory team. Establish whether there is a mechanism for you to request the allocation of a specific supervisor.

Setting off on the supervisor–student relationship

The simple message here is to start as you mean to go on. Even if you already know some or all of your supervisory team, we recommend that the first meeting begins with each party introducing themselves. For the supervisory team, this could include a summary of their research-related activity to date and areas of expertise. For the student, this could include an explanation of their academic/research activity to date, their preferred learning style, what they perceive their research skill-set to be currently and why they wish to undertake a doctorate (see Chapter 4). A lot can be learned during these introductions, even when people previously thought they already knew each other well. It is worth spending time discussing what the student and supervisors expect of each other. The supervisors' practice is likely to be shaped by their personal experience of being supervised themselves and the regulations of that particular institution (which may have been a different institution). Similarly, your expectations will be influenced by your experiences of being supervised (perhaps for Master's level study) and supervising other students. This is the time for all parties to clarify exactly what the institution's regulations stipulate regarding supervision.

Time should also be spent during this first meeting identifying potential challenges, particularly those associated with the supervisory team working in the same institution. This is not a case of predicting doom and gloom, but it is about being open and honest so that trust can be established and strategies can be put in place to ensure the best possible working relationship. Part of this may include agreeing ground-rules, particularly regarding professionalism and confidentiality. It is also helpful to clarify supervisory team and student expectations and preferred ways of working. Over time the nature of the student–supervisor relationship will naturally change. There will be times when a supervisor challenges the student to ensure they can provide a rationale for their choices. This may come as a surprise to the student if previous supervisory meetings have been more akin to a comfortable 'chat'. There will also be periods where a supervisor takes a lighter touch if they feel confident about the student's abilities and the way in which their doctorate is progressing. It is important to stress that supervisors and students are not required to become 'best friends' over the course of a doctorate. Although some friendships are established in this way, the key issue is that students and supervisors should respect, trust and feel comfortable with each other.

To help plan for your first supervisory meeting, undertake the following activity.

Activity 5.2

Identify what you would say about yourself at your first supervisory meeting. Be honest. Now is the time to acknowledge your skill-set and personal strengths as well as areas of weakness. For example, is time management a strength or a weakness for you?

Identify your expectations of your supervisory team. Reflect on what you think your supervisory team is likely to expect of you.

Case study 5.2

Zöe is undertaking her part-time doctorate in her home institution. She was delighted with the two supervisors she had been allocated. They were established and respected academics within the institution and both had a long track record of doctoral supervision. Their knowledge of research methodology was second to none. However, here lay a potential problem for Zöe, who felt she had previously 'got by' with a limited knowledge of research methodology. She recognised that she needed to acknowledge this at the first supervisory meeting and was relieved that, when she did this, both supervisors were supportive. In addition to the work that would form part of the Postgraduate Certificate in Research, Zöe's supervisors recommended some further reading and related activities for her to undertake to increase her knowledge base. However, it was made clear that the onus was on Zöe to do this.

Managing your supervisor(s)

Students 'managing' their supervisors is not a new concept (Wisker, 2008). As the student–supervisory team relationship progresses, the student should feel in control, or at the very least comfortable with the association. You should also feel that you 'own' your doctorate and that you are not being driven to undertake a study that a supervisor wants in order to address their personal agenda. A supervisor's role includes ensuring that the student's doctorate is 'on track', that they address the study aims and objectives and that they do not set out to do anything unethical, illegal, morally inappropriate or logistically impossible. There may, of course, be times when a supervisor challenges the student about their decisions. In such situations, they usually take on the role of 'devil's advocate' to ensure the student can provide a sound rationale for their plans and actions. However, supervisory meetings should be conducted in a supportive atmosphere and should not be combative.

In terms of managing your supervisor(s), some will require a lighter touch than others. You may already have a hunch about how likely this is to be the case, if your supervisory team is known to you. Managing a supervisor from your home institution may feel daunting, particularly if you already know them in a different context, but simple strategies can help:

- Find out from the outset your supervisors' preferred way of working. Based on this and your preferences, agree a pattern of working. For example, this could be that when sending your supervisors drafts of your work, you will send it to them a minimum of seven days before feedback is required.
- Think in advance of each meeting about the key issues that you wish to discuss. Your supervisory team may request that you send them a list of discussion points ahead of the meeting.
- Aim to start each meeting by summarising what you have done since the previous meeting. Identify the progress you have made with the actions agreed at the previous meeting.
- Take notes during the meeting and/or audio-record the meeting, as long as you have permission to do so.
- Towards the end of the meeting, summarise what you have discussed and use this opportunity to clarify any points.
- Identify your action plan going forward and specifically what you will do or provide feedback on at the next meeting. Also identify anything a supervisor will do before the next meeting: for example, to find the reference for a paper they have referred to or to email a contact who may be able to help you to recruit participants.
- Arrange the date, time and venue for the next meeting.
- After the meeting, provide your supervisory team with a summary of the key points discussed and the agreed action plan. Most doctoral colleges have a form that you can complete regarding this and will require that you also provide them with a copy (see below).
- If you are concerned that a supervisor will have forgotten to undertake agreed actions, a 'gentle reminder' a couple of days before the next meeting in an email may be helpful.

As indicated above, most institutions require doctoral students to complete and submit documentation about meetings to their supervisory team and the institution's doctoral college. This provides a record of the discussion at the meeting and the decisions made. This is also a useful way of keeping everyone up to date, particularly if a supervisor was unable to attend a particular meeting. If your institution does not require that you do this, then we suggest it a useful approach that you could implement (see the templates section of the online resources for an example).

We acknowledge that it can feel quite daunting employing these strategies initially. Being assertive with people you already know can be unnerving. However, you will feel more comfortable and confident as time progresses and it will soon feel normal. Your supervisory team will also almost certainly value this approach as you take responsibility for your learning and the development of your doctorate.

Being supervised by someone you know: What are the benefits?

As we have previously indicated, it is not necessarily a negative thing to be supervised by someone previously known to you. As the supervisor–student relationship continues, there are a number of potential benefits. These can include:

- A mutual understanding of the intricacies of the institution
- Having an understanding of the institution's perceptions of power, authority, hierarchy and expectations regarding patterns of behaviour and professionalism, which enables these to be acknowledged and addressed or strategies to be put in place to minimise or prevent their impact
- Mutual respect and trust
- The need for a shorter 'getting to know' period
- An innate shorthand about ways of working
- Feeling inherently at ease with each other
- The student feeling comfortable about disclosing confidential information.

Case study 5.3

Ned had thought long and hard about undertaking his doctorate and who might be best placed to supervise him. He had known Professor Davies for over a decade and they had previously worked together on a number of research projects. It meant they understood each other's preferred ways of working and were comfortable discussing issues of a more personal nature that may impact significantly on Ned's doctoral journey. This included the likelihood that Professor Davies would have to take a significant period of sick leave in the near future as well as the breakdown of Ned's long-standing personal relationship and

Ned having to negotiate access to his children. Knowing each other well meant that it was much easier to navigate these challenges and establish how supervision could be managed during these difficult times. As they both respected and trusted each other, they were comfortable speaking openly and honestly about any concerns, including those related to Ned's doctoral progress.

Being supervised by someone you know: What challenges may arise?

While all of the factors listed above may be benefits, misplaced assumptions can be counterproductive. The supervisor–student relationship necessitates working together closely over a long period of time. This can be six or eight years for part-time doctoral students, which can be longer than many other partnerships or friendships you may encounter. It is therefore likely that it is only over time that supervisors and students truly get to know each other. During this time, the student may disclose confidential information. The impact of knowing such privileged information may place a supervisor in a difficult situation and they may feel that they need to breach confidentiality. While this should not be done without the student's knowledge, it may in the longer term compromise their relationship both within and beyond the doctorate.

A number of other difficulties may arise that can impact the supervisor–student relationship in a negative way. Examples of difficulties include:

- A blurring of student–supervisor role boundaries
- Differing student–supervisor expectations
- Either party adopting a 'laissez-faire' attitude
- Unclear or contradictory supervisor guidance
- Excessive demands being made by the supervisor that exceed the capability of the student or are beyond the remit of the doctorate
- Lack of student engagement
- Supervisor feedback that is overly harsh, ambiguous or superficial
- Significant differences of opinion about the direction of the study
- Conflicts of interest about managing student commitments outside the doctorate (for the academic, this could include managing other aspects of their workload).

The effect of these situations can be magnified when the student and supervisors work in the same institution. Difficulties may be further increased if, outside the doctorate, the supervisor and student are working together closely or one is the line manager of the other. Any disclosure, by either party, regarding the challenges being encountered may be perceived as a slight or undue criticism that may extend beyond the doctorate.

Managing the situation when a student–supervisor relationship is compromised

While the aim should be to pre-empt a situation when the student–supervisor relationship is at risk of breaking down, this may not always be possible. The very fact that a student feels compromised may mean that they are unable to take action. Such a feeling may be magnified if the student and supervisor have a professional or personal relationship outside the doctorate. Nevertheless, unless someone else notices that the student is in difficulty, it ultimately requires them to speak up. Rather than raise their concerns with their supervisory team, the student may wish, in the first instance, to discuss the situation with a third party, such as the doctoral college. The underlying cause(s) of the difficulties will need to be established. These could include, for example, unrealistic supervisor expectations, gender issues, hierarchical factors or the failure of the student to acknowledge their academic limitations. In order for the student to continue their doctorate, a change of supervisor may be required. Although all parties involved may be concerned that this will lead to their having a poor track record, in many cases it will be in the best interest for all involved to make a fresh start. However, in some cases, supervisors and students are able to work through their difficulties and ultimately the relationship becomes stronger, as the following case study identifies. Sometimes you just have to be professional and get on with it.

Case study 5.4

Viv had worked alongside one of her supervisors (Wendy) for several years before she began her part-time doctorate nine months ago. Viv's second supervisor is external to the institution and only joins supervisory meetings periodically via social media. Viv was initially pleased to have been allocated Wendy, who is an experienced and successful supervisor. However, Viv soon felt that Wendy was taking an overly relaxed attitude to doctoral supervision. Wendy seemed to want to spend most of their supervisory meetings chatting about wider institution-related issues and discussing her own work-related problems over a cup of coffee in the canteen. Viv is now rapidly becoming frustrated and concerned that she is not progressing with her doctorate in the way that she should. Taking time out from her heavy workload for doctoral supervision is problematic for Viv and she therefore feels this precious time should be as productive as possible.

Ask yourself...

- What might be the reasons for Wendy's and Viv's differing behaviours and approach to doctoral supervision?
- How do you think Viv should tackle this situation?

Our thoughts about the possible explanation for Wendy's and Viv's behaviours and approaches to doctoral supervision can be found on the book's accompanying online resources.

How to tackle the situation

Here are our suggestions on the ways in which Viv could tackle the situation:

- Initiate revisiting the student's and supervisor's preferred ways of working and role expectations
- Agree a general format for supervisory meetings
- If either party feels that a more 'social' catch-up would be beneficial, arrange a separate meeting rather than use the supervisory meetings
- Ensure that the next supervisory meeting takes place in a more formal setting (such as a classroom)
- Request that the external supervisor participates in the next supervisory meeting
- Use a more formalised medium than social media for liaising with the external supervisor
- Email the supervisor a list of things Viv would like to discuss in advance of the next supervisory meeting
- Endeavour to take the lead at the next supervisory meeting: Viv could begin the meeting by summarising her progress to date and identifying what she considers to be the most pressing issues to be addressed
- At future supervisory meetings, take notes and/or audio-record the meeting to monitor progress more actively
- At the end of future meetings, summarise what has been discussed
- Identify an action plan going forward
- After the meeting, email the supervisors a summary of the key points discussed and the agreed action plan, and send a copy to the doctoral college
- Discuss workload and the allocation of study time with her line manager
- If the situation continues, discuss the situation with the doctoral college.

Managing the situation when the student or supervisor relocates

The possibility that either the student or a member of the internal supervisory team relocates during a doctorate is more likely when the student is studying part-time, simply because of the longer study period. The usual practice is that the doctorate continues in the institution where it was started. However, practical and logistical issues may make this impossible. If the student has relocated over some distance, they may wish to transfer their studies to a more local institution. This may require the student to negotiate the new institution's required regulations and procedures. For example, this will almost certainly require the student to acquire approvals from the new institution before the study can continue. A reconfiguration of supervisors is also likely to be needed to include a supervisor from the new institution.

If an internal supervisor relocates (or retires), they may be able to continue as the student's external supervisor, but it will depend on the regulations of the institution concerned. However, a new internal supervisor will need to be added to the team. Conversely, the student may decide to relocate also and transfer their doctorate to the supervisor's new place of work. Sometimes supervisors can put pressure upon a student to do this, particularly if the doctorate is related to their own body of work. However, if the student is an academic undertaking their doctorate in their home institution, they are unlikely to be able to easily relocate in order to follow their supervisor.

Whatever the final outcome, when either the student or the internal supervisor relocates it can be an unsettling and stressful time for the student, particularly if a partial or completely new supervisory team is required. New relationships will have to be established and the student may be fearful that a new institution or supervisory team will have different expectations, demands and procedures.

Case study 5.5

Karl had reached year four of his part-time doctorate when he secured a more senior post at an academic institution 200 miles away. Karl's family therefore relocated. His new employer made it clear to Karl that he was expected to transfer his doctorate to his new place of work. Karl was happy to do this. However, he was disappointed that in order to comply with the new institution's regulations, only one of his original supervisors was able to continue his supervision. His newly appointed internal supervisor was mindful of the potential impact of the transfer on Karl's doctorate and put strategies in place to support him. However, looking back, Karl felt the transfer had put his doctorate back by at least six months. His new supervisory team needed this amount of time to gel and he also had to complete the procedural requirements associated with the transfer.

Online/remote supervision

As we have identified elsewhere in this book, the recent international Covid-19 pandemic has created numerous challenges for everyone, and this includes doctoral students. Among these challenges is the impact on supervisory meetings. Many institutions have restricted or prohibited face-to-face interactions, such that all supervisory meetings are now carried out online or remotely. While this can undoubtedly be beneficial to some, for other doctoral students it may add to their feelings of isolation and their perception of a disconnect between themselves and the institution. It may be particularly problematic for academics who chose to undertake their doctorate in their home institution because of the advantage of direct accessibility of their supervisory team. There is no longer the chance of bumping into your supervisor in the corridor or at the photocopier, and so the opportunity for serendipitous supportive conversations is lost. Doctoral colleges and supervisory teams have worked hard to support students during these difficult times and your institution will hopefully have provided you with guidance, support and access to additional resources.

Guidance provided by Kumar et al. (2020) may also prove useful. Although written primarily for supervisors, doctoral students who receive online or remote supervision for whatever reason will also find their guidance valuable (for more, see the online resources). In their helpful systematic review, Gray and Crosta (2019) also explore some of the challenges and intricacies of online doctoral supervision.

As we conclude this chapter, it is important to emphasise that for most students undertaking a doctorate, their relationship with their supervisory team over the course of their studies is unproblematic. Students, including academics, who undertake their doctorates outside their home institution may need to navigate their way around procedures and systems that are unfamiliar to them. They will also have to spend time getting to know their supervisors and their preferred ways of working. However, the benefits may outweigh these factors in that the supervisory team is not likely to have a previous relationship with the academic and most certainly will not have any links to their 'day job'. Some people may prefer this arrangement, seeing it as a clear separation between their working relationships and that between the student and supervisor. There may be occasional 'blips' along the way but, in our experience, these are usually quickly and easily resolved.

While there may be additional challenges for academics undertaking their doctorate in their home institution, these can mostly be pre-empted if there is a clear action plan in place and a student–supervisor relationship that is based on honesty and respect. As with any working relationship, problems may arise from time to time, but these can usually be dealt with quickly and are speedily resolved. Time invested in making the relationship work is usually time well spent, ensuring an effective, professional experience for all concerned.

As a conclusion to this chapter, undertake the following reflective exercise.

Reflection 5.1

Reflect on what sort of a doctoral student you are likely to be, and what sort of a doctoral student you would like to be.

Identify what strategies you can put in place to ensure you are able to gain the most benefit from the student–supervisor relationship.

Identify the ways in which your supervisory team can best support you in order to facilitate the successful completion of your doctorate.

To access the online resources accompanying this chapter, please visit:
https://study.sagepub.com/harvey

Six

Navigating procedural challenges

Undertaking a doctorate can at times seem like a rollercoaster ride of ups and downs. The 'highs' can be a great confidence boost and motivator. In contrast, the 'lows' can leave a student feeling frustrated, despondent and possibly disengaged from their studies. However, if this does occur, it is important to recognise that these lows do not necessarily indicate a lack of ability or resilience. Instead, they are a common feature of most doctoral studies. It is very rare for someone to sail through their doctorate from beginning to end with everything going according to plan. We suggest that anyone who tells you that was the case for their doctorate is either being economical with the truth or, with the best of intentions, is trying to encourage and motivate you. Alternatively, they may just have a short memory. Like the pains of childbirth, it is amazing how quickly some people forget! Although there may be those who create the impression that their doctorate was trouble-free, it is more realistic to acknowledge that it is rarely a smooth journey from start to finish. Indeed, the troughs can sometimes feel overwhelming, leading to demotivation and perhaps, in extreme cases, thoughts about discontinuing the doctorate.

In this and the next chapter, we aim to identify the challenges that you may encounter on your doctoral journey and provide strategies that will help you to ride out any lows. These strategies will enable you to continue with your doctorate so that you can enjoy the highs and proceed to successful completion. The two chapters should therefore be read in conjunction with each other. In this chapter, we will identify some of the possible procedural and work-related factors that can lead to doctoral 'lows'. In Chapter 7 we will explore some of the more personal and emotional factors that can have a negative impact on doctoral progression. Of course, these elements are interrelated: procedural factors can impact on emotional well-being and vice versa. However, we feel that to acknowledge their significance, both factors deserve focused attention. Potential strategies to overcome doctoral delays will be suggested in both chapters and excerpts from case studies will be used as illustrations. Throughout both chapters, you will be directed to a range of tools and resources for ongoing support that can be found on the book's accompanying online resources.

Possible doctorate lows

There are a number of procedural and work-related factors that can cause a student to feel a dip in enthusiasm and motivation about their doctorate. Juggling the demands of workload while endeavouring to maintain doctorate progression can be particularly challenging for academics undertaking a part-time doctorate.

Procedural delays

Student frustration can occur when procedural aspects of the research component of their doctorate do not go according to plan. These delays are usually caused by issues that are beyond their control. Sometimes procedural aspects of the research process can take longer than expected. This might include awaiting decisions from an ethics committee, awaiting confirmation of permission to access a study site or waiting for feedback from reviewers. Delays may also be encountered organising a temporary contract if this is required in order to access a study site.

If these sorts of delays occur, it may be that the expectations of both the student and the supervisory team were initially unrealistic and timelines need to be revised. Nevertheless, doctoral students often feel under pressure to be constantly moving forward and these delays can be frustrating. An academic undertaking a part-time doctorate may have less time to follow-up delays as they endeavour to manage other commitments associated with their professional life, especially if they need to speak to a particular person on a specific date or time. Finding the right person to liaise with can also be a challenge and it is not uncommon to feel that you are going around in circles. In addition, getting the balance between chasing decisions or information while not pestering people can be tricky. Forward planning and ascertaining who you need to speak to and the best way and time to contact them will help. However, sometimes you just have to be patient and wait. Keeping detailed records about who you have liaised with, when and what they advised may prove useful in subsequent discussions on the matter. In the worst-case scenario, such evidence may be valuable if you have to make a request for an extension for your studies.

Delays in the conduct of the research

Delays in the conduct of a study most commonly occur when the student is dependent on a response from other people. Delays most frequently arise in relation to participant recruitment, maintaining contact with participants, data collection and obtaining required resources. The dependence on the input of others often means that the student has limited control over the situation. However, there may be strategies that can be put in place to minimise or address the causes of the delay and these will now be explored.

Tackling delays in participant recruitment

The recruitment of participants can sometimes be slower than anticipated. It may be due to initially unrealistic expectations. While we would all like to think that people will be queuing up to take part in our research, it is rarely the case. In some instances, participants will need to be recruited via a third party or gatekeeper. This in itself can be time-consuming, and if the other person is time-pressured or is not as committed to your study as you might like them to be, then there can be additional delays. The time allocated for participant recruitment in the research plan should therefore be realistic and, if relevant, adjusted to anticipate timescales if the student is undertaking their doctorate on a part-time basis. Recruitment rates should also be carefully monitored. Under the guidance of the supervisory team, amendments may be required to the participant inclusion/exclusion criteria, participant documentation and recruitment strategies. Note that if these sorts of changes are proposed, amendments to the study protocol, along with research governance and study site reapprovals, will almost certainly be required before the changes can be implemented. If participant recruitment continues to be slow, it would be wise to review the overall research proposal. For example, is there something about the study which means that potential participants are reluctant to take part? It may be prudent to amend the focus of the research slightly.

Academics who are part-time doctoral students can find participant recruitment challenging, particularly if they plan to do it themselves. Fitting this into an already busy schedule can be problematic, especially if multiple visits to the study site(s) are required to finalise recruitment. It may be worth considering alternative strategies, which may include, for example, someone recruiting on your behalf. Clearly, you and your supervisory team would need to weigh up the pros and cons of adopting this strategy.

Case study 6.1

The approvals for Cora's study required her to give prospective participants a minimum of 24 hours to decide whether they would take part. To identify potential participants Cora enlisted the help of Hesta and Claude at the study site. Cora ensured that they were familiar with the study's inclusion/exclusion criteria and were aware of Cora's availability. Hesta and Claude made arrangements for Cora to meet potential participants to discuss the study and to explain what taking part would involve. Cora returned to the study site the following day to see if the potential participants were willing to take part and, where relevant, to secure informed consent and to arrange for data collection. This process, including the involvement of Hesta and Claude, was outlined in Cora's study approvals.

Fortunately, the study site was a short distance from Cora's place of work, so she was able to travel quickly between both places. Nevertheless, during the participant recruitment phase, Cora was at the study site on numerous occasions, often daily and usually in the early evening after work or at the weekend.

Managing delays in maintaining contact with participants and data collection

Doctoral students may encounter delays as they await a response from participants. It might include waiting for prospective participants to confirm that they are willing to take part in the study. There may also be delays as the student waits for participants to confirm their availability for data collection (for example, via a face-to-face interview). The timescale over which to follow up participants can be difficult to gauge. Some participants will welcome a 'gentle reminder' to respond, while others may consider attempts to contact them to be pestering. At the point of initial contact, it is therefore important to establish the participant's preferred method of maintaining contact with them (for example, by phone, text or email) and the best time of day to contact them. You should have a clear follow-up strategy which indicates the number of times and over what period of time attempts will be made to contact participants. This should be outlined in your study protocol and approvals. It is important to remember that for some participants, their lack of response may be their way of indicating that they do not wish to take part in the study.

Students may encounter delays as they wait for participants to provide data (for example, photographs, completed questionnaires or diaries). To minimise the risk of this occurring, it is wise to ensure that procedures are as straightforward for the participant as possible (for example, by providing stamped addressed envelopes or a secure website where they can upload their data).

Maintaining contact and experiencing delays receiving data from participants can be particularly problematic for students undertaking longitudinal studies. Specific strategies to minimise or address this problem may therefore be useful. It could include making occasional telephone calls to participants or sending newsletters or birthday cards. These can act as prompts to maintain engagement with the study. If you plan to use such strategies, they should be documented in your study approvals and outlined to participants at the start of the study. For academics undertaking a part-time doctorate, finding the time in their busy schedule to maintain contact with participants in these ways can be a particular challenge. Having a clear plan at the outset of the study will be invaluable, with reminders to contact participants at key timepoints.

It should be noted that some participants may not provide their data because they feel uncomfortable about saying they no longer wish to participate in a study. Almost all types of study involving human participants will have some level of drop-out. As a consequence, most supervisors will advocate some degree of 'over recruitment' of participants. For quantitative studies, the calculation of sample size will probably involve a power calculation (Harvey and Land, 2017). It is important to remember that all researchers are dependent on participant goodwill and cannot 'demand' their commitment to the study. While some participants with the best of intentions may initially agree to take part, they are sometimes unable to ultimately do so, for a variety of reasons. In some studies, participants may be offered an incentive to take part or have their expenses covered. However, there can be ethical concerns about such practices (Resnik, 2015), and doctoral students usually have limited resources from which such incentives or participant expenses can be funded. Resources that provide guidance on covering participant expenses can be found on the book's online resources accompanying this book.

Supervisory meetings should include a review of the progress of data collection. Under the guidance of the supervisory team, amendments may be required to data collection strategies. For example, is there something about the chosen method of data collection which means that participants are reluctant to take part? Amendments may also be required regarding the strategy for maintaining contact with participants. Note that if these sorts of changes are proposed, amendments to the study protocol, along with ethics and study site reapprovals, will probably be required before the changes can be implemented.

Academics who are part-time doctoral students can find arranging face-to-face data collection challenging. Fitting this into their academic workload can be problematic, especially if travel time is required in addition to that needed for the actual data collection. Ensuring adequate time is set aside for maintaining contact with participants and data collection can be easier said than done. With regard to the former, a short amount of time set aside each day may prove useful. Regarding data collection, it may be worth considering someone doing this on your behalf. You and your supervisory team would need to weigh up the pros and cons of adopting such a strategy. With regard to both maintaining contact with participants and data collection, it is essential that you set out with a realistic research plan that fully recognises the time that this is likely to take. It is always safer to overestimate than underestimate.

Case study 6.2

Floyd was undertaking a part-time doctorate while working as a full-time academic. He quickly began to find that maintaining contact with participants was much more time-consuming than he had initially anticipated. His concern about this was heightened when preparing for his next supervisory meeting. He became aware that he had 'lost' contact with two participants. He realised his strategies for record-keeping were inadequate and discussed more effective ways of doing this with his supervisory team. It was agreed that he would set up email alerts to himself at key timepoints to remind him to contact participants. He set time aside every Monday and Thursday to review the state of progress with each participant. On most occasions, this review took only a matter of minutes.

Delays in the provision of essential resources

Some studies require the provision of equipment or materials in order for the research to be conducted. If this is the case, it should be determined and wherever possible put in place before the study commences. It may involve setting up a contract with a supplier, which in itself can be time-consuming. This is often not the remit of the doctoral student and instead will be undertaken by a member of the supervisory team or the doctoral college. Deciding who ultimately should pay for equipment or resources is not always straightforward and needs to be established before your study protocol and approvals are finalised. If an essential piece of equipment cannot be purchased, you will have to make alternative plans for your study.

Despite everyone's best efforts, having everything in place before a study begins is not always possible, for example if funding is to be released annually. There may therefore be a delay as the student awaits delivery of replacement resources. Alternatively, during the course of a study, the supplier may have to be changed, which will necessitate a new contract being set up. Forward planning, with realistic timescales in place, should minimise any delays.

Case study 6.3

Winifred's part-time doctorate required the manufacture of a device which was to be tested in a randomised controlled trial. It was hypothesised that the device would support the development of mathematical skills in primary school children. A contract was set up with a manufacturer in which it was agreed that a set number of devices would be made per year, for which the supplier would be paid annually. However, part-way through the study, the manufacturer went out of business. A new supplier had to be found and a new contract set up. It took six months to resolve and during this time Winifred's data collection had to stop.

On some occasions, delays in conducting a study are caused by external factors that impinge on the progress of the research. In this instance, a doctoral student almost certainly has no choice but to 'sit it out'. At the time of writing this book, there is no better example of such a factor than the international outbreak of Covid-19 (see below). During this time, most face-to-face research activity has been stopped except in a few exceptional cases.

For an academic undertaking a part-time doctorate in their home institution another factor that can cause doctoral delays is trying to balance the requirements of their workload against the need to maintain doctoral progression. It is an issue over which many academics feel they have little or no control. Consequently, we have decided to explore this issue along with other procedural challenges.

Managing academic workload while undertaking a doctorate

You will note as you read through this section that we refer to 'study time' rather than 'study leave'. This is deliberate, because time for study should be part of the configuration of your academic role. To refer to this time as 'leave' sends out the wrong message. It is not a 'holiday' or 'time out'; it is part of doing a doctorate. Indeed, there is nothing more galling on your return from study time than a well-meaning colleague asking *'have you had a nice holiday?'*. Most institutions assign all academic staff an allocation of study time for continuing professional development. We advocate that the amount of time allocated should be increased for those undertaking a doctorate and should be pro rata for those undertaking part-time study.

Academics studying for a doctorate will almost certainly be under significant time pressure associated with other aspects of their roles and responsibilities within the institution. Competing professional demands can mean that their own academic needs are given a lower priority by themselves or others, and sometimes by both. At times, their needs may not be recognised at all. Academics may encounter challenges regarding role boundaries in terms of both how they see themselves and how others regard them. Are they an academic studying for a doctorate or a doctoral student who happens to be an academic? There is not a uniformly 'right' or 'wrong' answer to these questions and a person's perception of themselves is likely to change at varying stages of the doctorate. However, the academic's perception, and that of others, will have an impact on many factors, including how their overall academic workload is managed. Uncertainty about role boundaries can be magnified for academics undertaking a doctorate in their 'home' institution.

If you are an academic undertaking a doctorate, to enable you to explore this issue carry out the following activity.

Activity 6.1

Consider the following questions and give an explanation for each of your responses.

- Do you regard yourself as an academic studying for a doctorate or a doctoral student who happens to be an academic?
- Do your colleagues and peers regard you as an academic studying for a doctorate or a doctoral student who happens to be an academic?
- Does your line manager regard you as an academic studying for a doctorate or a doctoral student who happens to be an academic?
- Do the students who you interact with regard you as an academic studying for a doctorate or a doctoral student who happens to be an academic?
- Do you anticipate any of the above perceptions changing over time? If so, what factors do you think will influence this change?

Some of the groups identified in the above activity may be currently unaware that you are undertaking a doctorate (possibly your students or perhaps your work colleagues). There may be a particular reason for this: for example, you may have chosen not to disclose that you are undertaking a doctorate because you do not think it is relevant for them to know this. However, if those around you are to understand and support your navigation through your work pressures, then we suggest that they should know about your doctorate.

Look at your answer to the first question. Your response will be determined by what you currently regard as the most important of the two elements. Do you think that the ways in which you have to date managed your academic roles and responsibilities and doctoral progression could be explained by your response to this first question? Look at your response to the second, third and fourth questions. Is there a pattern here? Do you think that the ways in which you have been supported to manage your academic roles and responsibilities and progress with your doctorate could be explained by the ways in which you portray yourself to others? Or perhaps by the ways in which others choose to regard you (for example, your line manager)?

An academic's perception about their doctorate and the way that others regard them can be influenced by the overall ethos of the institution or department. Some organisations will place higher prestige on academics working towards a doctorate than others. The former may result in transparent strategies being put in place to manage workload for at least some, if not all, of the doctorate. However, while this might be regarded as being an enlightened approach, it can bring with it associated pressures, such as the expectation of successful completion within a defined timeframe. For academics working in institutions that do not take this enlightened approach, although the intention among colleagues, peers and line managers may be to be supportive, they will probably feel that the academic's workload and the 'business' of the institution are more important than your doctorate. This ethos will often be driven by institutions vying for business with each other (Boncori and Smith, 2020). It is too simplistic to suggest that changing the perception of the student and those around them will immediately solve workload problems. The determining factor may be the ethos of the institution and the attitude of the key players, such as line managers. This will impact upon the ways in which doctoral funding, study time and resources to support doctoral study are allocated. Ultimately, it may come down to the student making the best of the situation and articulating their needs when they can.

Case study 6.4

As we noted in Chapter 2, at the time that Cora commenced her doctorate, her line manager Helen was unsupportive. Helen questioned the value to the team and the institution of Cora achieving her doctorate. While her line manager's attitude was frustrating, it made Cora all the more determined to find a way to continue her studies and ultimately to succeed. Generally, Cora preferred to keep her doctorate a private matter at the institution, and her line manager's attitude enabled her to do this.

Look at your response to the final question in Activity 6.1. In our experience, the emphasis will almost certainly shift over the course of your doctorate (Goodall et al.,

2017; Boncori and Smith, 2020), particularly if the doctorate is being undertaken on a part-time basis when there is a wider timeframe for changes in perception to occur. As time progresses, doctoral students often become more assertive and determined to ensure that their individual needs are met. To some extent, pressure to complete on time will be a factor, along with a desire to reach the finishing post.

Activity 6.2

What factors may influence the changes in perception (both yours and that of others) identified in Activity 6.1?

Which of these can you influence or be proactive about instigating?

Strategies to manage academic workload

One of the key challenges for an academic undertaking a doctorate is managing their professional workload while endeavouring to move forward with their studies. As we have seen earlier in this chapter, dealing with procedural doctoral delays can be all the more challenging for a student who has other professional responsibilities. Taking the study time to which they are entitled can also be problematic for academics. Clark and Sousa (2018) advocate that if an academic does not have control of their time management, then someone else will. While they were writing about time management more generally, we suggest that the same principle applies to academics taking their study time.

Activity 6.3

Ask yourself: Who has 'control' over the allocation and taking of your study time? We will come back to your response to this question later in the chapter.

There are a number of strategies that an academic can employ to manage their professional roles and responsibilities to ensure that they have time set aside to work on their doctorate. While some of these strategies may apply to all doctoral students, they are particularly directed at academics undertaking a part-time doctorate in their home institution. Here are some of our suggestions:

- Clarify with your line manager and doctoral college at the start of your doctorate exactly how much study time you are entitled to, noting that this allocation may change at faculty or department level over time.
- Identify what works best for you in terms of taking study time. Do you prefer to take single days? Or is it better for you to take consecutive days or blocks of time? Note that what works best for you may change during the course of your doctorate.
- Draw out a timeline of your academic workload and map this against the proposed timeline for your doctorate. Highlight any dips in your workload where you could focus on your doctorate. Negotiate with your line manager *now* to protect this time. Highlight peaks in your workload where it would not be sensible for you to try to work on the elements of your doctorate that require focused attention. Negotiate with your line manager *now* to secure study time during the dips in your workload on the understanding that you will take less study time during the peaks.
- Put your study time in your calendar and treat it as if it were annual leave. In other words, when you are asked to participate in other work activities during this time, respond by saying that you are not available.
- Do not apologise for taking study time.
- Say no to work that is outside your current roles and responsibilities. There can be the temptation to take on other work because it seems interesting (or is possibly a distraction), but you need to be disciplined and focus your attention on the 'here and now' of your doctorate.
- If you are able to do some work on your doctorate while at work, do this in a different setting, such as the library, a colleague's office or a postgraduate student area. It will make you less accessible to others and will also enable you to focus your attention on your doctorate.
- If you have to cancel study time (for whatever reason), immediately reschedule it.
- Keep meticulous records of the study time that you have taken, including time that you had to cancel (for whatever reason) or reschedule.
- Negotiate with your peers to cover aspects of your work. This could be a reciprocal arrangement with fellow doctoral students. Take this plan to your line manager.
- Explore the possibility of securing Visiting Lecturers to cover aspects of your role. If you know of individuals who would be interested in taking on some aspects of your work, bring this to the attention of your line manager.
- Take whatever opportunity you can to attend activities organised by the doctoral college, such as writing retreats, viva preparation or other professional development activities. It will bring your studies back into focus, reinforcing to yourself and others that you are doing a doctorate.
- Review your current roles and responsibilities. Is there anything about your current situation or circumstances that you could usefully incorporate into your doctorate?
- Explore the possibility of securing a sabbatical. You may have to apply for external funding to do so and you will need to discuss it with your line manager and doctoral college (see Chapter 7).
- Employ the help and support of your supervisory team, line manager, doctoral college or senior faculty personnel as appropriate to enable you to secure the study time to which you are entitled.
- Use formal doctorate reviews and individual performance review processes to identify the study time you have taken and that which you were unable to take.

Some of the above may seem tough and will require you to be assertive. You may want to avoid following formal grievance or complaint processes, but ultimately it may be in your best interest to do so if you have been unable to take the study time to which you are entitled, particularly if you know that other academics (both in your faculty and the wider institution) have less difficulty taking their allocated study time. If you take this route, you will need to identify the *real* reason why you have not taken your allocated study time. There may be laudable reasons why you have been distracted by other aspects of your role, such as not wanting to let the students or your colleagues down. Your responses to the questions in Activity 6.1 may also be an important factor. If others (probably your line manager) genuinely have control over the allocation and taking of your study time then some of the strategies identified above may help you to tackle the problem. You ultimately may have to take the issue to a higher authority, such as your head of school/department/faculty. However, and this is one of those uncomfortable questions that we periodically have to pose, *is it the case that you perceive that others have control over your study time when in reality this is a convenient excuse for you not taking it?*

Not taking your study time will not do yourself, other academics undertaking a doctorate now or in the future, or your institution any favours in the long run. Your institution has invested in you and delaying completing your doctorate may have consequences for both you and the organisation. For example, doctoral completions are a measure included in the Research Exercise Framework (REF, 2019). You therefore have a key role to play in advocating for yourself. Also, do not forget that you are a role model for other academics who might be considering undertaking a doctorate in the future.

Dealing with the 'really big stuff'

As we have identified earlier in the chapter, sometimes factors beyond your control impact on your doctoral progression. The international Covid-19 pandemic is a good example of this, as most face-to-face research was immediately put on-hold. In recognition of this fact, many institutions gave all doctoral students a blanket extension of, for example, six months. However, there are other far-reaching factors that may delay your progression. For example, the regulatory body associated with your discipline may announce an unexpected imminent inspection and you are deemed to be the only person who can deal with it. Alternatively, you may have arranged study leave cover with a colleague who is unexpectedly on sick leave for an extended period, or who leaves the institution. In these situations, it may at first be tempting to try to work through these additional challenges and continue with your doctorate. This may be possible if you are absolutely certain that it will be for a short period and that any study time that you have been unable to take will subsequently be honoured.

However, timescales have a tendency to slip. What may initially have appeared to be a short-term problem may extend into something much bigger and longer lasting. We therefore advocate that you deal up front with these sorts of situations when they first become apparent. Consult your supervisory team, doctoral college and line manager and negotiate the best plan of action for you. Sadly, not all line managers are as supportive as we might like. While they inevitably have a responsibility to ensure that the work of the department or team is covered, the institution has also made a commitment to you in supporting your doctorate. You should absolutely not have to take unpaid leave or sick leave in order to complete your doctorate. If you find yourself in a position of stalemate, you and your supervisory team should pursue the matter with a higher authority, such as head of school, faculty or doctoral college. If you feel that you do not have the head space to work on your doctorate during this time, the best course of action may be for you to take an interruption from your doctorate (see Chapter 7). However, be mindful that this may simply push the problem of your workload to a later date. Alternatively, you may feel that, despite everything, you would prefer to carry on with your doctorate. Only you will know what is right for you. We would strongly advocate, if you do continue with your studies, that you clearly document any study time that you have taken and any that you were unable to take so that outstanding study time can be taken at the earliest opportunity.

Case study 6.5

Floyd felt that the strategy he had developed to maintain contact with his study participants was successful (see above). However, some months later the Covid-19 pandemic had a sudden impact on his doctoral progression. All programmes at Floyd's institution had to be very quickly reconfigured for online delivery. The institution made a unilateral decision about the reallocation of workloads. This meant that Floyd's academic responsibilities suddenly increased exponentially. All face-to-face research at the institution was immediately stopped. However, Floyd felt that he wanted to try to continue working on his doctorate. In consultation with his supervisory team, it was decided that he would 'revisit' his literature review during this time. Floyd found the best way for him to do this was to work on his doctorate from 05.00 to 07.00 before the rest of the household woke up. During this time, he read and annotated papers and created thematic tables for his revised literature review. With the help of his supervisory team, Floyd negotiated with his line manager that any study time scheduled during this period of reconfigured workloads would be carried over to a time when Floyd would be able to take it.

Within this chapter, we have explored some of the procedural challenges and those associated with academic workload that may be encountered when undertaking a doctorate. We have identified strategies to overcome or forestall these challenges. It must be acknowledged, however, that there may be other perhaps more uncomfortable reasons why a student is unable to progress with their doctorate. Some of the possible reasons will be addressed in the next chapter, which deals with the more personal and emotional factors that can have a negative impact on doctoral progression. We will also identify strategies to help maintain momentum and motivation in order to facilitate the successful completion of your doctorate.

> To access the online resources accompanying this chapter, please visit:
> https://study.sagepub.com/harvey

Seven

Navigating personal and emotional challenges

In the previous chapter we explored some of the procedural challenges that may be encountered during a doctoral journey. In this chapter we consider some of the more personal and emotional factors that can have a negative impact on doctoral progression, including the adjustment to the academic requirements of a doctorate and the personal challenges this can present. We will then consider maintaining momentum and motivation with your doctorate, coping emotionally with low points, and we will look at possible strategies to help you move forwards with your doctorate. Excerpts from case studies will be used as illustrations. We have also included in this chapter some short reflective pieces from current and recent doctoral students. As was the case for the previous chapter, you will be directed to a range of tools and resources for ongoing support that can be found on the book's accompanying online resources.

Adjusting to the academic requirements of a doctorate

The step up from Master's to doctoral-level study can be more difficult for some students than others. 'Doctoral-ness' can be a mysterious concept, particularly in the early days of a doctorate. Studying and writing at doctoral level therefore commonly causes anxiety in most doctoral students (Goodall et al., 2017). Writing at doctoral level comes more naturally to some than others. Grappling with the requirements of doctoral-level study in the early days may indicate that there has been a lack of information or guidance from the doctoral college or supervisory team about what is expected. It may also suggest an initial lack of understanding on the part of the student about what a doctorate involves. Alternatively, and much more likely, it may indicate that the student needs a period of adjustment to achieve the required academic level. This can take longer for some than for others and, in some cases, it is not achieved until towards the end of the doctorate. The key roles of the supervisory team and the doctoral college are therefore to ensure that students are aware of what they are taking on and to support the development of academic skills.

It can be a shock for a student to discover that their academic writing skills do not meet the expected level, especially if they have previously been a 'high achiever'.

Activity 7.1

Think back to the time before you started your doctorate. What did you think doing a doctorate involved academically? How would you have defined 'doctoral-ness' at that time?

What do you now think doing a doctorate involves in terms of the academic requirement? How do you now define 'doctoral-ness'?

Some doctoral programmes involve early formative or summative assessment, which in part may highlight academic difficulties. Lower than anticipated achievement or academic failure should raise awareness in both the student and supervisory team of the need for additional support or that other strategies should be employed.

Although it might be assumed that academics will innately have an understanding of the requirements of a doctorate, they can feel just as, or perhaps even more, anxious than other students about achieving the required standard. Academics may feel additionally vulnerable if they are undertaking their doctorate in their home institution, where judgements are being made about their achievements by supervisors who are also their peers and colleagues. Lower than anticipated achievement, identification of gaps in their knowledge or failure of early academic work can be challenging (Boncori and Smith, 2020). It can cause the student to feel exposed, particularly if they are in a cohort with their peers. It may be easier to conceal academic struggles if the doctorate is undertaken in an external institution.

Case study 7.1

Hattie is an academic undertaking a part-time doctorate in her home institution. The doctoral programme required her to undertake the in-house Postgraduate Certificate in Research. She attended the first few sessions of the taught component, but workload commitments meant that she had to stop attending. Hattie felt this was the right thing to do because in the sessions she had attended, she did not feel that she had learned anything new. Hattie felt comfortable with the requirements of the two assignments, both of which had to be passed before she could proceed with her doctorate. Hattie did not seek tutorial support from her supervisors and they assumed that because she had not asked for guidance, she did not need any support. When the results were published, Hattie was horrified to discover that she had achieved a borderline pass for one piece of work and had failed the other.

Addressing the academic challenges of a doctorate

As we discussed in Chapter 4, the start of a doctorate is the time for all students to be completely honest about their skill-set. For example, do you need to update your literature searching skills? Are there aspects of research methodology about which your knowledge base is limited? Do you find time management a challenge? The start of your doctorate is the time to acknowledge areas that you need to work on. Rather than admitting to your weaknesses being a negative experience, it can be liberating, especially when the strategies that are subsequently put in place lead to successful outcomes. We advocated in Chapter 4 that you develop a personal development plan at the beginning of your doctorate. If, for whatever reason, you have not done so, we recommend that you undertake the following activity.

Activity 7.2

Undertake a SWOT analysis of your current research and academic knowledge and skills using the template on the book's online resources. Be completely honest with yourself.

From this SWOT analysis, develop a personal development and action plan for one aspect of your research knowledge and skills that requires development.

As we have seen in Chapter 5, supervisors have an important role to play in enabling a student to develop the required knowledge and academic skills to achieve their doctorate. Assumptions should not be made about a student's knowledge base or research skills. This may mean that during supervisory meetings in the early months of the doctorate that your supervisory team probes your level of knowledge and suggests areas requiring development. The supervisory team should, where appropriate, support the development of action or personal development plans to ensure that the agreed goals are realistic. The plans should be reviewed by the student and supervisory team at regular intervals.

Managing the adjustment to the academic requirements of a doctorate also requires complete honesty between the student and their supervisory team. As discussed in Chapter 5, the student needs to feel comfortable that issues discussed will remain confidential. These meetings provide an opportunity for discussion and for promoting the student's critical thinking skills. You may feel that your supervisory team is being overly challenging, but this may be because they are trying to facilitate the development of your doctoral-level thinking. Conversely, if you feel that your supervisory team is not challenging you sufficiently, you should say so.

It must be acknowledged that writing at doctoral level is usually something that develops over time and it is often only when a student looks back at their earlier work that they can see how their writing and thinking have developed. In the short term, there is no getting away from the need for students to read extensively in order to develop their understanding of 'doctoral-ness' and to enhance their critical thinking and writing skills. This is not a part of the doctoral journey where shortcuts can be taken.

Case study 7.2

Having received feedback on her two assignments, Hattie met with her supervisory team. Initially, Hattie felt embarrassed and then became antagonistic as they discussed her work. Hattie's supervisors explained their feedback, giving examples of areas that needed development. Hattie was not receptive at this point to what her supervisors were saying. Consequently, the meeting ended abruptly and it was agreed that they would meet again the following week.

By the time of the second meeting, Hattie felt calmer and had reflected on her prior assumptions about her level of knowledge, her critical thinking skills and her supervisors' feedback. At this second meeting, they agreed an action plan, which indicated both what Hattie would do and what support her supervisors would provide.

Maintaining momentum and motivation

Struggling emotionally with doctoral lows can adversely affect endeavours to maintain both momentum and motivation. Maintaining momentum so that your doctorate continues to move forwards can be challenging, especially when your study is not progressing in the ways that you feel it should. Maintaining motivation can also be problematic, particularly when you feel disheartened about your doctorate. These two factors are, of course, interrelated in that one can lead to the other. However, in the first instance, we feel that they are different issues and so we will explore them separately.

Maintaining momentum

As we have previously identified, all doctorates have peaks and troughs. The impact of undertaking a part-time doctorate on the need to maintain momentum adds to the challenge. Working on the doctorate in a fragmented way can at times feel counterproductive. It may take a whole day of precious study time to find the point that you had reached previously. In addition, some more focused and detailed aspects of a doctorate require more than one day of concentrated effort in order to move forward. In these instances, consecutive days of study time will be required in order to maintain momentum. Consequently, overall doctoral progress may appear slow or indeed feel as though it is coming to a complete halt. Sometimes you cannot 'see the wood for the trees'. As highlighted in the previous chapter, it can be particularly frustrating if external factors over which you have no control, such as waiting for confirmation of ethics committee approval or permission of access to a study site, lead to delays. For academics, the lack of clear definition between aspects of the doctorate and their 'day job' can also cause them to lose sight of their overall doctoral progress.

Maintaining motivation

For any doctoral student, maintaining motivation, especially during the low points, can be daunting. Again, for part-time doctoral students maintaining enthusiasm for their studies can be especially onerous. At times, students cannot see the point of what they are doing and aspects of their doctorate may appear mundane and overly time-consuming. It is not uncommon to begin to doubt your ability and to become fearful about being 'found out'. This is sometimes referred to as 'imposter syndrome' (Bothello and Roulet, 2019) or 'monsters of doubt' (Hawkins and Edwards, 2015). These feelings may lead doctoral students to question why they began their doctorate in the first place. Fitting a doctorate around an already busy workload can be demotivating, but can be compounded by the fact that the longer a doctoral task is avoided, the harder it is to eventually pick it up again. It is also not uncommon to put off tackling aspects of a doctorate about which you lack confidence, such as submitting documentation for ethics committee approval, or feel you have gaps in your knowledge, such as about a specific aspect of research methodology.

Developing an action plan may help you to maintain both momentum and your motivation. It will also enable you to provide evidence to your supervisory team that, among all your other commitments, you are also are working on your doctorate. In developing an action plan, you should set realistic and achievable goals (see Chapter 4, pp. 47–48). Do not be over-ambitious about timeframes. It may be tempting to suggest that you can turn around large pieces of work in a short period of time. You may be lured into agreeing to unrealistic timeframes because you want to appear to be a 'good student'. However, not meeting overly ambitious timeframes is likely to add to your stress levels, rather than reduce them. For most doctoral students, small, 'bite-sized' goals are more helpful than large-scale, longer-term goals (see Chapter 4, pp. 47–48) and your supervisory team should help you to set achievable goals.

As will be explored later in this chapter, applying for or negotiating a sabbatical may also boost your motivation. It will provide a period of dedicated and uninterrupted time during which you can become fully immersed in your doctorate.

You are not alone

When a doctoral student hits a low point, there is a tendency for them to assume that they are the only person to have ever had negative feelings about their doctorate or to have come to a standstill with their work. However, we know from our own doctoral experience that this is not the case. As we have already indicated, low points are a natural part of almost every doctoral journey.

Students may be fearful about disclosing feelings of despondency about their doctorate, especially for academics who are undertaking their doctorate in their home institution. There may be many reasons why such a student feels that they should create the impression that all is well, and some of them are encompassed in the next case study.

Case study 7.3

Raymond, whom we first met in Chapter 3, feels that he has come to a complete standstill with his doctorate. However, he is reluctant to raise his concerns with his supervisory team because he fears that it would lead to closer scrutiny of his work and progress to date. Raymond has for some time been 'covering his tracks' and has fallen into the habit of frequently rescheduling supervisory meetings at the last minute. Raymond feels the pressure of the commitment that the university, his supervisory team, line manager and colleagues have made to him regarding funding, the provision of study time, supervisory support and covering aspects of his workload, and the provision of more general support is having a negative impact on the situation. One of the main motivators for Raymond starting his doctorate was to help him secure a promotion within the institution. He now questions whether this is of such importance to him. He feels there is no one within the institution to whom he can confidentially disclose his feelings and concerns.

Other reasons why a doctoral student may feel reluctant to disclose their true feelings about their doctorate may include:

- They anticipate that they will soon be 'back on track' and so prefer to try to muddle through
- Acknowledging that all is not well will contradict the persona that they have previously created within the organisation: for example, that they are a 'starter finisher', that they have high academic credibility or that they are resilient
- They do not want to appear weak or academically incompetent
- They feel unable or unwilling to disclose factors within the organisation that have caused or affected their struggles: for example, agreed study time has not been honoured or the lack of support from their line manager
- They feel unable or unwilling to disclose factors outside the organisation that have caused or affected their struggles: for example, ill health in their family or relationship difficulties
- They do not want to disclose to family and friends that they are struggling, for whatever reason.

Activity 7.3

If you are creating the impression that all is well with your doctorate when this is not actually the case, think about why this might be. Do any of the reasons that we have identified in Raymond's case study or in the list above apply to you? Are there any other factors that apply to your situation?

As we have identified, doctoral students may be fearful about voicing their worries and concerns to their supervisory team, doctoral college or their line manager. However, not disclosing these feelings can mean that difficulties escalate to the point where the student feels they have no other option than to interrupt or discontinue their doctorate. In the hope of preventing this situation from occurring, in the next section, we offer some strategies that may prove useful.

Strategies to facilitate moving forward

The exact strategies you can deploy will depend on which stage of the doctorate you have reached and the reasons why you have come to a standstill.

Activity 7.4

Be completely honest with yourself and make a list of the reasons why your doctorate has come to a halt. What are the factors that have disrupted your momentum and motivation?

Categorise your reasons into different groups. For example, are they institution-related, supervisory team-related, factors external to the doctorate or personal reasons?

Identify one thing that *you* could do in relation to each of the groups that would enable your doctorate to move forwards.

Identify one thing that *someone else* could do (for example, your supervisor or line manager) in relation to each of the groups that would enable your doctorate to move forwards.

Remind yourself of what you have already achieved

This is not about being smug or complacent. It is very easy to focus on what you have not done, rather than on what you have achieved. This is one of the subsidiary reasons why keeping a reflective journal is important (see Chapter 4). Looking back to the start of your doctorate will enable you to see just how far you have come. You may have already overcome what may have felt like insurmountable problems. Look at what you did in the past to maintain momentum and motivation. Remind yourself of your resilience and persistence. You also need to trust your judgement and be proud of what you have already achieved.

Reflection 7.1

If you have kept a reflective journal during your doctorate, look at the early entries.

What have you learned about yourself by revisiting these earlier accounts?

What strategies have previously worked for you when you have encountered problems or challenges in the past (both within and outside the doctorate)?

Look at the phases or aspects of your doctorate that went well and analyse why this was the case.

Activity 7.5

Revisit your SWOT analysis. What knowledge and skills do you have that you are not currently employing that could enable you to move forwards? Identify why are you not currently employing this knowledge and these skills.

Taking a diversion

In the short term, diversion tactics can help, so try focusing on another aspect of your doctorate for a while. For example, revisit your literature search or review, spend some time formatting tables and graphs, collate documentation for your appendices or submit an abstract for a conference. Some 'quick wins' will help you to feel you are moving forward and will fuel your motivation. However, you need to be careful about deliberately or unwittingly employing diversionary tactics over the longer term because this is likely to prevent you from tackling the real obstacle.

Seeking support

There is no shame in asking for help and guidance if you feel you have lost motivation or momentum. What formal or informal support networks do you have or that you can access that could help you? One of the ways to identify your potential support networks is to create a network diagram or eco-map (Vodde and Giddings, 2000; Hill, 2002). On a piece of paper, place yourself at the centre of a circle. Within the circle, note down potential sources of support that you have both within and outside your institution. Position those that you are most likely to access closest to you, and those with which you have more minimal contact further away. An example of a completed support diagram can be found on the book's accompanying online resources.

Activity 7.6

Complete a support network diagram or eco-map to establish your sources of support both within and external to the institution.

- Are there sources of support that you are not currently accessing? If so, why not?
- Are there sources of support that you have accessed more than you previously realised?

The exact nature of the support that you may access will depend on the cause(s) of your current problem and the context at the time. For example, if the cause is a specific aspect of the research process or the need to develop your academic writing skills, then you need to tackle those issues. This is the time to be honest with yourself, as the problem is unlikely to go away on its own. Draw on the knowledge and expertise of colleagues around you. You may be able to find someone with knowledge of a specific research method or a member of the library or information technology team to help you. If you are an academic doing your doctorate in your home institution and feel that you want to seek help outside your immediate working environment, explore some potential sources of support in another faculty or department where you are less well known.

If your struggles are because of a more general lack of motivation or momentum, sometimes the best person to help will be someone who has been there before. Is there someone you know who has recently completed a part-time doctorate? They may agree to take on the role of a 'buddy' or mentor. It can be helpful if the person is someone outside your immediate sphere, for example, from a different department, school or faculty. While some students prefer the 'splendid isolation' of doing a doctorate, sharing experiences and learning from each other can be invaluable (Hay and Samra-Fredericks, 2016; Mantai, 2017). In addition, if you feel that ultimately you will need to raise a concern with your supervisory team, line manager or doctoral college, a buddy can be a useful listener if you want to practise what you will say.

Does your doctoral college or institution have a support network for doctoral students? Some institutions hold regular informal meetings for doctoral students, such as a monthly breakfast club or a lunchtime doctoral forum. In addition to providing emotional support, such gatherings can also be a forum for sharing resources. There is no point in reinventing the wheel when you are constantly pressured for time. While these groups often do exist, they are usually open to all doctoral students, including full-time and external students. It is of course important that the support needs of all students are addressed. However, meeting the needs of a mixed group of students can sometimes be problematic. Academics studying a part-time doctorate in their home institution may not feel comfortable sharing their experiences with those on different programmes and other students may regard them as being 'insiders'. It is therefore worth considering whether a group specifically for academics studying a part-time doctorate in their home institution can be established.

— Case study 7.4 ——————————————————————

The Doctoral Forum meets every month on a Friday lunchtime and is specifically for academics undertaking a part-time doctorate either at the institution or externally. The forum provides a safe place to discuss issues confidentially. It provides an opportunity for academics to share their doctoral experiences and challenges, and the strategies they have used to overcome them.

Guest speakers are sometimes invited, and on other occasions attendees take turns to lead the discussion. Sometimes the discussion is more informal and the attendees appreciate that the Doctoral Forum gives them the space in which to do that.

The forum recently had to move online as a consequence of the Covid-19 pandemic and it has become an even more important way of combating feelings of isolation. Attendees have commented that fitting in the online forum into their busy schedule was easier than endeavouring to attend a face-to-face event.

Later in this chapter, a current doctoral student reflects on a range of his experiences, including the value of the doctoral forum to him.

Networking

Networks both within and external to your place of work can be invaluable. Does your place of work have a research group that you could join? These are often either subject- or research method-specific. Explore whether there are research groups in another faculty that would be appropriate for you to attend. Widening your networks can provide you with ideas and opportunities that will reinvigorate your motivation and momentum.

You may already be part of an external network relating to your professional background. Does this network have a research or doctoral group that you could join? Can your colleagues recommend a network that you could join? Sharing ideas, experiences, advice and resources can be useful. Interfacing with people outside your immediate circle can also be refreshing. Opportunities to attend external meetings will also give you time away from your academic role and place of work.

Activity 7.7

List the organisations related to your profession that you either already belong to or could join. Investigate whether they have a research or doctoral group that you could join.

Taking a sabbatical

A possible strategy to reinvigorate your motivation and gain some momentum with your doctorate is to take a sabbatical. It can provide you with a clear run of time to focus specifically on your doctorate. During the sabbatical, aspects of your workload should be allocated to others and everyone should be clear about who will be doing what. You should investigate what arrangements are in place regarding sabbaticals at your institution as there is likely to be an application process. Alternatively, you may be able to secure external funding (see Chapter 3). You should discuss the timing of a sabbatical with your supervisory team, the doctoral college and your line manager before you apply. Should you secure a sabbatical, you owe it to yourself to use the time wisely. The temptation to deal with work-related issues during this time should be avoided. If, however, you find that your line manager or work colleagues expect you to continue with aspects of your work during your sabbatical, you should raise your concerns with your supervisory team, the doctoral college and line manager as a matter of urgency. If you have been unable to take all of the time that was previously agreed, you may be able to extend your sabbatical.

Getting words on the page and dealing with writer's block

Most doctoral students encounter writer's block at some point. Consequently, we have included it here and we identify strategies to deal with the problem. Writer's block is when the words just will not come. You may find yourself attempting to write a particular sentence over and over again or feel as though you are staring into the abyss.

First, think about the setting in which you are trying to work on your doctorate. If you are at your institution, move away from your desk to a different setting, such as the library, a colleague's office or postgraduate student area. Doing so will make you less accessible to others and will minimise distractions, enabling you to focus your full attention on your doctorate. It will also represent a physical break from your usual workspace, a signal to yourself to leave your 'day job' behind and that work on your doctorate has begun. If you are working from home, it may help to move to a different area or room from where you do your academic work for the institution to work on your doctorate. Again, this will indicate to yourself that work on your doctorate has begun. Whether at your institution or at home, do not look at work emails during this time.

If the words just will not come, rather than waste a whole day looking at a blank page or computer screen, there are a number of things you can try. Some of the activities described in the 'Taking a diversion' section earlier in this chapter may help, such as sorting your references or formatting tables and charts. Alternatively, in some instances, giving yourself the day off may be more productive in the long run.

However, if you really need to get words down on the page, then try to say out loud what you are attempting to express in writing. You can do this on your own or you may find it useful to ask someone to help you, such as a member of your supervisory team. It may also be useful to record and playback what you want to say. Alternatively, generate a list of key facts that you need to cover in bullet-point format and then build these into sentences. Rather than being fastidious about each individual word, just get something down on the page. Do not allow yourself to start tweaking or correcting; you can come back on another occasion to do that. Do not let yourself become distracted by other seemingly urgent tasks, such as a pile of ironing or mowing the lawn, until you have at least got some writing done, even if it is in a very basic format.

In the longer term, writing retreats can provide a conducive environment in which to focus your attention on writing.

Case study 7.5

Mary, a lecturer and current doctoral student, writes here about a technique she has developed which has helped her to 'get words on the page':

> I have started to record the chats and supervisions I have with my supervisors because I am much better at verbally articulating some ideas than writing them. I have then been simply transcribing some of this so that it gives me a basis for further writing and filling in the gaps with references, etc. I find writing something I have already said word-for-word quite therapeutic. It makes me feel as though I have produced something and I then don't need to do the thinking process twice.

Do you need a doctorate rethink?

We are assuming here that you want to continue doing a doctorate, but that you have become stuck with some aspect of it. If you are undertaking a professional doctorate, it may be that the programme is taking you down a path that you no longer wish to follow. If this is the case, you need to have an open and honest conversation with your supervisory team and the doctoral college. You may be able to switch programmes, but this will be at the discretion of your institution.

Alternatively, you may have become stuck with some aspect of the research component (whether you are doing a professional doctorate or a PhD by research). In order to move forwards, sometimes you need to review your current position and perhaps take a sideways step. You need to consider: is this the study that you *really* want to do?

It is possible that you have unintentionally deviated from your initial research idea. Sometimes this can happen when you get caught up in the ideas and work of others. To some extent, exploring other viewpoints is part of the normal process at the beginning of a doctorate and is a way of refining and confirming your ideas. However, it can become counterproductive if you become overwhelmed by other options and consequently lose sight of what you originally intended to do. Your supervisory team should help you to keep 'on track'. It can also be helpful to periodically remind yourself of what you set out to do and what your original research question(s) are. Getting the foundations right will enable you to build a solid and robust doctorate.

In a similar way, when conducting a preliminary search and review of the literature some students find that their reading becomes unfocused and distracted. Sometimes people refer to 'over-reading' or 'reading too much'. We would contest this view because exploring a few 'blind allies' is part of the process of confirming exactly what the focus of the study should be. However, we do acknowledge that difficulty can arise if the student becomes bogged down in literature, some of which may not be useful or relevant. Consequently, they cannot see how to move forwards in order to finalise their research question(s) (see Figures 7.1 and 7.2).

For many doctoral students the process of moving from their original research idea to their finalised research question(s) can be portrayed diagrammatically as a diamond shape (Figure 7.1). Students begin with their research idea. Then, when exploring the literature, they become exposed to material that takes them beyond the specific focus of their original thoughts but that still broadly relates to their initial idea. From this wider body of work, they narrow the focus down and this culminates in their finalised research question(s). These finalised questions may have moved away slightly from their original idea.

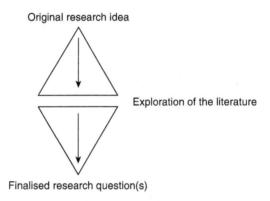

Original research idea

Exploration of the literature

Finalised research question(s)

Figure 7.1   Successfully moving from research idea to research question(s)

Conversely, for some doctoral students, the process of moving from their original research idea to their exploration of the literature can be portrayed diagrammatically as a pyramid (Figure 7.2). The student begins with their research idea. However, when attempting to explore the literature relating to this idea, they become exposed to more and more material that has less or no relevance to their initial idea. Consequently, they lose sight of the original focus and cannot move forward from the vast amount of literature that they have generated. In this situation, the only way forward is to go backwards; to go back to the original research idea and to start again. Seeking guidance on literature searching would also probably be prudent.

As we have identified several times, if you are doing a part-time doctorate, you are in it for the long haul. If you have lost sight of your original idea, such that your heart is not in the research component, then your doctoral journey will be much more challenging. Do you have an opportunity now to tweak your proposal to realign it with your ideas and areas of interest? There does come a point where it

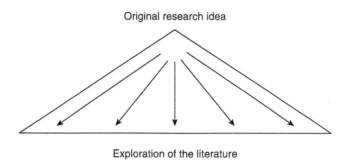

Figure 7.2 Unsuccessful attempt to move from research idea to research question(s)

is harder to change track and if you have already secured doctoral college and ethics committee approvals and permission to access a study site, then this might be trickier. In the first instance, you need to discuss this as soon as possible with your supervisory team. Something for you to consider is: have you been persuaded to deviate from your original research idea?

Sometimes doctoral students are 'guided' away from their original research idea by their supervisory team or doctoral college. This may be for legitimate reasons if the initial research proposal was unachievable within the required timeframe or was unethical. However, sometimes the motives and agenda of others come into play. If you are being steered away from the research that you really want to do, then it is not surprising if you are now feeling a dip in energy or enthusiasm for the study. You need to have a frank and honest discussion as soon as possible with those who have manoeuvred you to the position in which you now find yourself. It may be that they have not clearly articulated why your original ideas should not be pursued. You need to hold on to the fact that this is *your* doctorate. As such, you may need to negotiate a compromise or revert completely to your original ideas. In more extreme cases, you may need to change the configuration of your supervisory team (see Chapter 5). Part of doing a doctorate is about making choices and providing a rationale for these choices. It is not about always being told what to do. While this might be liberating for some, it can be quite challenging for others, particularly for those whose previous experiences of academic study has not included an element of choice.

Do you need to change institutions?

Some students reach the point where they feel that the only way that they can move forward with their doctorate is to change institutions. We advise against this being a knee-jerk reaction if at all possible. You need to carefully consider this option and be absolutely sure that it is the right thing for you to do. You will need to ensure that the new institution can accommodate your needs and you should establish whether your current allocation of study time and funding will continue to be honoured. You also need to find out about the doctoral processes and procedures of the new institution as these may be different from those to which you are currently accustomed. Also be mindful that you will almost certainly need to acquire research governance approvals from the new institution. This will be particularly important regarding the transfer of research indemnity insurance arrangements. To revisit the pros and cons of undertaking a doctorate in your home or an external institution, see Chapter 3. As an alternative to changing institution, a more prudent strategy may be to change members of your supervisory team. Issues relating to changing supervisors are explored in Chapter 5.

Taking a break

In managing dips in motivation and momentum, when determining the right strategy for you, the priority is that you take care of yourself. This is particularly important if doing the doctorate is having a negative impact on your well-being or that of your family, your friends or your life outside the doctorate. It can be easy to lose perspective, so you need to take care of the essential components of your life and invest time in yourself. Is the doctorate the 'be all and end all' of everything? A short 'timeout' period may be what you need. A 'timeout' does not need to be a formal interruption of your studies. Give yourself a break for a week or two. Treat yourself. Do things in your personal time that you enjoy and that have no connection whatsoever with your doctorate. Often a short break enables you to see the way forward. If taking a break means that you come back to your doctorate feeling refreshed and reinvigorated, then it will have been time well spent. When you do get back to your studies, think about whether the activities you have recently engaged in could be incorporated into your doctorate or work schedule to enable you to have a better work–life balance.

It may be that you need to take a more formal break from your doctorate. You will need to discuss the process for arranging an interruption of your studies with the doctoral college and your supervisory team. There is no shame in asking for a break. Pressing the pause button may give you the headspace to review other issues, such as your academic workload or to deal with challenges that you are currently facing outside your doctorate. However, it is worth being mindful that the longer the break, the harder it can sometimes be to return. Your doctoral college may have specific strategies for dealing with such matters, but it is worth developing an action plan for the period of interruption. Supervisory teams are also often willing to meet with students informally during the period of interruption, if the academic regulations permit it. Of course, you may need to take a break for other reasons, such as ill-heath or maternity/paternity leave. If so, the issues outlined above will also apply.

Start as you mean to go on

We are aware that much of the content of this chapter will appear to have a negative focus. However, we have endeavoured to be realistic about what doing a doctorate can be like and the specific additional challenges that an academic doing a part-time doctorate in their home institution will encounter. Rather than wait for problems to arise, it is far better to forward plan. It is prudent to have strategies in place from the beginning, for example, to manage your academic workload or to access sources of support. Implementing restorative measures part way through a doctorate, while not impossible, can be a challenge. Starting as you mean to go on establishes your mindset and your ownership of your doctorate. It also sends a clear message to your supervisory team, colleagues, line manager and the doctoral college about the ways in which you intend to pursue your doctorate. It must, however, be acknowledged that in order to be proactive, you need self-awareness of your current strengths and weaknesses and the strategies that are mostly likely to be effective for you. You need to be honest with yourself about the circumstances in which you work most effectively. Remember that what may be right for your peers who are currently undertaking their doctorate, or what worked best for your supervisory team, will not necessarily be right for you.

We conclude this chapter with an excerpt written by an academic about dealing with the challenges of doing a part-time doctorate.

Case study 7.6

Francis is a lecturer and current doctoral student. He writes:

> If I had to say anything it would be please don't feel guilty or beat yourself up. Whenever I start to analyse what I haven't managed to do, I then find it harder to do anything at all. Don't put yourself under any pressure to achieve anything in particular. However, if things are really difficult because of work or family commitments, then just try to accept that now is perhaps not the time and no one is going to blame you for that.

> My message is do what you can when you can and forget about the rest. ... The one tip I have is to remember that this is an iterative process in which we all learn and grow. As with all growth, it is dependent on what is going on around us and within us and may even direct us where we were least expecting. Hopefully and thankfully, it is always towards the light, which may be flickering, dim or just embers, but it will burn bright again soon ... this too will pass.

> I think the one tip that springs to mind is to talk to others, even if you feel behind or an imposter. The doctoral forum and attending one of the Postgraduate Researcher sessions earlier in the week have been helpful in creating a community and being able to listen to others.

In this and the previous chapter we have explored some of the procedural, personal and emotional challenges commonly encountered when undertaking a doctorate. These can of course be interrelated in that procedural challenges can lead to personal or emotional ones, or vice versa. In both chapters we have identified strategies to overcome or forestall these challenges. It is fair to say that attaining a doctorate can be rather like climbing to the top of a peak. It can be a real scramble at times and you may feel that others are putting obstacles in your way or that you are slipping backwards. However, with some resilience and forward planning, it is possible to negotiate these challenges. Others have done it before you, so there is no reason why you cannot do it too. Just think of the view when you get to the top!

To access the online resources accompanying this chapter, please visit:
https://study.sagepub.com/harvey

Eight

One stop to go: Preparing for thesis submission and the viva

In most universities, the viva or oral examination is an integral component of the doctoral examination process, in conjunction with the thesis. This is irrespective of the type of doctorate being undertaken, whether the student is an internal or external candidate or whether the candidate is studying full-time or part-time. The fact that most universities are explicit in stating that a student cannot fail a doctorate outright without having undertaken a viva or equivalent examination testifies to the importance of this component of the assessment process. However, the way in which the viva is conducted and examined may vary according to the type of doctorate, the regulations of the institution and the country in which it is undertaken.

This chapter begins by discussing the finalisation of your thesis. The purpose of the viva will then be clarified. We offer guidance on viva preparation, which should be undertaken throughout the doctorate (see Chapter 4). We believe that 'starting with the end in sight' applies here (see the online resources for a template of a Gannt chart). In this chapter, we emphasise that preparation requires careful consideration and planning throughout the programme of study and is not something to be left until the final stages. The chapter goes on to discuss the selection of examiners, particularly in the situation where an internal examiner is required from the same organisation as the candidate. The chapter concludes by discussing the viva itself and strategies to manage the process. Throughout the chapter, excerpts from case studies are used as illustrations. Activities are suggested and reflection points are posed to assist the reader's thesis submission and viva preparation. A range of tools and resources for ongoing support are also identified.

There is a wealth of material available to support doctoral students in writing their thesis. These resources include developing academic writing skills and demonstrating attainment of the required academic level (Bolton and Rowland, 2014; Nygaard, 2015; Kornuta and Germaine, 2019). Resources also identify what examiners look for in a doctoral thesis (Hodgson, 2020). Rather than reinvent the wheel, our aim in the following section is to provide practical guidance on preparing your thesis for submission (there is also an online resource to help you).

Preparing for thesis submission

Most institutions require students to notify them of their 'intention to submit' before the anticipated submission date. It enables the doctoral college to commence the examination arrangements (see below, 'appointing the right examiners'). You and your supervisory team should check with the doctoral college in good time what the requirements are for your institution. Your supervisory team should advise you when you should submit this notification.

The most important advice we can give you regarding that actual thesis submission is to follow the institution's instructions on the required format, processes and procedures. The institution will have guidance on how the document should be presented, whether you should submit electronic and/or hard copies, whether an anti-plagiarism report is required (see below) and what documentation should accompany the submission. You should follow these instructions to the letter. Do not assume that what your friends, colleagues or supervisory team were required to do for their doctorate will apply to you. Regulations change over time and often vary between institutions. If hard copies of your doctorate are required, ensure that you factor in time for printing, binding and delivering them to the doctoral college.

Some institutions or doctoral colleges require the finalised document to be reviewed by an internally appointed 'critical reader' prior to submission. The arrangements for this will vary. Sometimes the supervisory team organises it; in other cases the doctoral college will make the arrangements. It may be the case that the critical reader will also undertake the mock viva (see below). If you are involved in the process of appointing or agreeing the appointment of a critical reader, do not be tempted to opt for a friend or colleague whom you know will automatically give you positive feedback.

The critical reader should provide their feedback in a professional and constructive manner. The supervisory team and student should then review the feedback in the context in which it has been given and make decisions about any suggested changes. Receiving feedback from a critical reader can have both positive and negative consequences for the student. If the feedback is on the whole encouraging, the student can move forward to the submission of their final thesis with confidence. There is, however, the possibility that some of the feedback will be negative, which may be particularly difficult for the student if the critical reader is a friend or colleague. The possibility of encountering this sort of situation should be considered before the critical reader is appointed. Dealing with feedback that is largely discouraging may mean that the supervisory team and student have to make some uncomfortable decisions, such as rewriting some sections, which may in turn delay the submission. However, it is important to remember that the critical reader's suggestions are exactly that. They do not all have to be implemented, and so the supervisory team and student should decide which suggestions are acted on and which are not. If your institution does not have a critical reader system, discuss with your supervisory team whether it would be prudent to arrange for a critical reader yourselves.

Note that the institution may require you to run an electronic copy of your thesis through anti-plagiarism software immediately prior to submission. The report generated by the software may need to be included with the documentation accompanying your submission. You may also require supervisory team signatures on this and accompanying documentation. You should ensure that time for all these aspects is factored into your schedule. You should also ensure in advance that required signatories will be available at the appointed time if 'wet ink' signatures are required.

If you are an academic preparing to submit your thesis, think about the guidance that you give to students about assignment submission. Almost certainly, this guidance will apply to you now as you prepare to submit your thesis:

- Follow the institution's requirements for the format and presentation of the thesis.
- Do not underestimate the amount of time that you will need to finalise the document for submission.
- Allow sufficient time for proof reading.
- Ensure that you have followed the institution's referencing guidelines.
- Check that the references cited in the text are in the reference list and vice versa (even if you have used referencing software).
- Ensure that the appendices listed in the text are included in the document in the correct order.
- Ensure that the table of contents is correct.
- Check that you are consistent throughout the thesis regarding format, terminology and use of abbreviations.
- Ensure that you tell a coherent 'story' throughout the thesis; it can be quite easy to deviate away from the intended focus.
- Check that you have been consistent in the numbering of headings and sub-headings.
- Check that the chapters link together.
- Check in advance of the day set aside for printing that your printer works and that you have sufficient ink.
- Follow the institution's exact submission procedure.

Case study 8.1

During Zöe's part-time doctorate, she had encountered a number of personal and professional challenges that had caused various unanticipated delays. As a consequence, the end of Zöe's registration period was rapidly approaching. Her thesis had to be submitted in three days' time, but she felt that she still had sufficient time to meet the deadline. On the day that she had planned to run her thesis through the anti-plagiarism software, the institution's systems crashed. Although Zöe sought help from the IT department, they were busy trying to resolve institution-wide problems. It took a further 48 hours before she could generate the report which required her supervisors' 'wet ink' signatures. At this point, Zöe discovered that one of her supervisory team had been unexpectedly called abroad and was not contactable. In extreme distress, Zöe consulted her lead supervisor, who was able to negotiate alternative arrangements for Zöe's thesis submission with the doctoral college.

In our experience, we have seen that students can have mixed feelings about actually submitting their thesis. There will be a sense of relief and joy at having submitted the work. However, many students find it hard to 'let go'. There is the temptation to keep tweaking the thesis, but this can in time become counterproductive. There is a real risk of undoing the good work that has already been done. The supervisory team should be vigilant of the student encountering this scenario. Sometimes supervisors will need to 'strongly recommend' that the student stops tweaking their work and submits the thesis. Conversely, some students may wish to submit their work before the supervisory team feels it is ready. If the supervisory team and student have established a trusting and professional relationship during the doctorate, they should be able to work together to resolve the situation. However, in some cases the student may elect to go against supervisor guidance and submit anyway. Ultimately, it is the student's decision to submit. A final scenario may occur when both the student and supervisory team recognise that the thesis is not as they would like it to be, but the student has to submit because they are rapidly running out of time to meet the required cut-off date for submission (as in Zöe's case study above).

Having submitted the thesis, viva preparation now begins in earnest. Before we go on to explore viva preparation in detail, we would like to clarify what a viva is or, perhaps more importantly, what it is not.

What is a viva?

The doctoral viva, or viva voce, is an oral examination. In most countries, the viva is an integral part of the doctoral examination process (Rees et al., 2019; Hodgson, 2020). The viva is conducted by the doctorate examiners and it takes place after they have read and made judgements about the candidate's thesis. The length of time between thesis submission and the viva will vary according to the institution and examiner or candidate availability, but it is typically six to eight weeks (it can be much longer if coordinating everyone's availability is problematic). Generally, the viva is conducted face to face, but there may be some situations where one or more of those involved have to participate via the internet. It is preferable that online vivas are avoided because technical difficulties on the day have the potential to add to everyone's stress levels. Nevertheless, in difficult circumstances, such as those in 2020 when the international Covid-19 pandemic meant face-to-face vivas were impossible, online vivas proved to be eminently possible.

The number of examiners required will vary according to the type of doctorate and the institution. Most commonly, there will be two or three examiners, at least one of whom will be from the academic institution where the doctorate has been studied (known as the 'internal' examiner). In addition, there will be a Chair from the institution where the doctorate has been undertaken. The Chair's role is to oversee the proceedings to ensure that the institution's regulations are followed and to make sure that a fair and balanced viva takes place. The Chair does not usually participate in the viva, as they generally will not have had access to or read the thesis. However, in some institutions the internal examiner also takes on the role of Chair.

In addition to the candidate, the examiners and the Chair, some institutions allow a member of the student's supervisory team to attend the viva. The final decision about this should be left to the candidate. Some prefer to 'go it alone', while others find the supervisor's presence to be supportive. There can be an additional dilemma for students who have two (or more) supervisors. It can sometimes be difficult to choose one over the other. In this situation, some institutions permit the attendance of more than one supervisor. If the supervisor does attend, they should not participate in the viva and should be positioned in the room out of the candidate's and examiners' line of vision. The supervisor's role is usually to take notes of the examiners' questions and the candidate's answers. These notes can be extremely helpful post-viva, especially if amendments to the thesis are required. The following case studies offer contrasting views on supervisor attendance.

Case study 8.2

As the date for Ned's viva approached, his supervisor, Professor Davies, said to him 'you don't want me to sit in on your viva, do you?' Up to this point, Ned had not realised that his supervisor's attendance could have been possible. Ned initially felt obliged to say 'no' but, on reflection, recognised that he did not want his supervisor to be present. He now believes that Professor Davies realised this and was making it easier for him to say so.

Case study 8.3

Parveen was very pleased that her supervisor, Ralph, had agreed to attend her viva. They met before the viva and over a coffee they chatted about unrelated issues. They talked about their forthcoming holiday plans and films they had recently seen. Although during the viva, Parveen could not see Ralph, she felt his presence was a comfortable reassurance. As she answered some particularly challenging questions that they had previously rehearsed, Parveen felt sure that Ralph was smiling and nodding as he sat behind her.

Activity 8.1

What do you feel about one of your supervisory team being present during your viva? What would be the pros and cons *for you* of a member of your supervisory team being present?

Although uncommon in the UK, some institutions and countries hold the viva 'in public', that is, in front of an audience, or the candidate delivers a lecture to a panel (Rees et al., 2019). The audience consists of invited colleagues, friends and the family of the candidate. This type of viva is usually only conducted when the examiners have already approved the doctorate. The public viva is therefore a formality to confirm the doctoral award.

Activity 8.2

What would be the pros and cons *for you* of your viva being undertaken 'in public'?

The actual format of the viva can vary. For example, some institutions require the candidate to give a formal presentation at the beginning. It is therefore essential that the candidate and supervisory team are clear about the institution's required format to ensure appropriate viva preparation takes place. During the viva, the examiners will ask the candidate about various aspects of the thesis, the research process, the dissemination strategy and the candidate's experiences of doing the doctorate. The candidate will also usually be given the opportunity to explain any amendments that they would like to make to their thesis. The length of the viva can vary, but it usually lasts one to two hours. We consider the conduct of the viva and candidate preparation in more detail later in the chapter.

What the viva is not, or what it should not be

Perhaps inevitably, a doctoral student approaching their viva will often be regaled with viva horror stories by those who deem themselves to be 'in the know'. These are usually apocryphal tales or accounts that have been 'embroidered' for retelling and they should therefore be ignored.

The focus of the viva should be the candidate's thesis. It should not, therefore, be an arena for the examiners to champion their own personal agenda on the topic to the extent that the views of others (including the student) are dismissed without being given due consideration. The careful appointment of examiners should prevent such a scenario from occurring (see 'Appointing the right examiners' below). In situations where the questioning during a viva does start to become aggressive or the focus switches to a difference of opinion between the examiners, the Chair should step in, which is why the appointment of a Chair, who will advocate where appropriate for the candidate, is also important (see below).

The viva should also not be a forum for the candidate to blame others for any flaws in their work. While explaining the context in which decisions were made may be important, the candidate should ultimately take ownership of the thesis and the study that it is describing.

The purpose of the viva

The main purpose of the viva is for the examiners to be satisfied that the candidate (rather than anyone else) has done the work. The candidate should therefore be able to demonstrate that they understand their study and can articulate where the work is positioned in relation to wider research on the topic. Evidence of the candidate's understanding of their work will include their being able to explain and give a rationale for what they have done. Thus, the candidate 'defends' the decisions they made, and thereby their thesis. The examiners will also use the viva as an opportunity to clarify aspects of the thesis that they feel are unclear or to discuss issues that they feel are not adequately addressed. However, the viva is not just about discussing any negative aspects of the candidate's work. The examiners will also discuss the work's strengths. In addition, the viva can be an opportunity for the examiners to discuss with the candidate their professional development during the doctorate, the support they have received, their plans for the dissemination of the findings and potential post-doctoral work. The viva therefore provides the candidate with the opportunity to talk in depth about their study and their experience of doing a doctorate. It may be the first and last opportunity they will have for such a detailed discussion about their work with anyone.

Preparation for the viva

For some doctoral students, the viva is a taboo subject and they take the view that 'if I don't talk or think about it, it will go away'. However, as we have previously identified for most doctorates, it is an integral element of the examination process. It is important to emphasise that viva preparation should not begin at the final stages of the doctorate. In many ways, preparation for the viva should begin on day one. However, we acknowledge that most students, particularly those taking the part-time route, find it difficult to look that far into the future at the start of their 'journey'. Nevertheless, keeping detailed accounts of decisions and actions from day one (usually in the form of a reflective journal) (see Chapter 4) and throughout the doctorate can be a useful resource to revisit as the viva approaches. Without such a journal, it can be difficult to remember why certain decisions were made five or six years ago or the context in which those decisions were made.

Some institutions have progression points at key stages of the doctorate whereby the student's progress to date is reviewed and a decision is made whether or not they may continue their doctorate. These doctoral progression points may include a requirement for the student to present aspects of their work and to respond to questions posed by a panel of reviewers. Although it can feel daunting at the time, this approach can be invaluable preparation for the viva as it happens within what should be a supportive environment. Similarly, students may be required to attend an ethics committee meeting in order to gain approval for their study or to meet with gatekeepers to gain access to a proposed study site. These situations will provide opportunities to gain experience talking about the research and, in particular, giving a rationale for aspects of the research process and their decision-making. Conference presentations are also important elements of viva preparation. For academics, talking about your research in your teaching can be an invaluable experience. A few challenging questions from students may give a useful insight to aspects of your research that you need to be able to articulate or defend more clearly.

As you work through your programme of study, it is worth considering who your doctorate examiners might be. Not thinking about this until the end of your doctorate may lead to rushed decisions being made based purely on potential examiner availability. You may, for example, encounter the work of an expert in the field (topic and/or methodology) who could ultimately take on the examiner role. We are not suggesting that you skew your study to suit their agenda, but it may be worth being at least mindful of their stance and to ensure that you develop an understanding of their full body of work as you proceed through your doctorate. When it comes to the appointment of both internal and external examiners, the institution's criteria usually preclude someone with whom the candidate has worked in a direct way, or who has previously participated in assessments as their doctorate has progressed. Knowing who your examiners are likely to be may therefore help you to make decisions during your doctorate that will not ultimately prohibit their appointment. For more detailed consideration about the selection of doctoral examiners see 'Appointing the right examiners' later in the chapter.

As the viva approaches

Occupying your time between the submission of your thesis and the viva can be a challenge. Your doctoral college may run specific viva preparation workshops or you may wish to access similar events that are delivered by an external institution. You may find this type of activity helpful. However, some candidates prefer to prepare quietly on their own with the support of their supervisory team. Some supervisors recommend that students use the time between thesis submission and their viva to work on papers for publication. It has been reported that there is an upward trend in the number of doctoral students publishing during their doctorate (Horta et al., 2018). While it will not be appropriate for everyone, working on papers during the period between thesis and viva can be a constructive activity which will necessitate revisiting aspects of the doctorate.

Peer mentoring or support can be useful as a candidate's viva approaches (Knight et al., 2018). Some institutions automatically put such arrangements in place. If this is not the case in your organisation, it may be worth exploring the possibility or making your own arrangements. Guidance and support from someone who has recently successfully completed their viva can be invaluable. Ask your doctoral college or supervisory team if they know of people who have recently completed doctorates who would be willing to do this. Alternatively, approach colleagues yourself informally. Such mentoring and support does not necessarily need to be a formal or lengthy arrangement. An occasional chat over a cup of coffee may suffice.

It is important that time is set aside for viva preparation. There can be a tendency for family, friends, colleagues and line managers to think that the 'work is done' with the submission of the thesis. However, study time should continue to be allocated and it is particularly important for academics undertaking a part-time doctorate in their home institution. Colleagues and managers should not use the period of time immediately post-thesis submission as an opportunity to increase an academic's workload.

As you get closer to the viva, it is worth considering examples of viva questions and giving some thought to your possible answers (you can see examples of viva questions on the online resources). You may wish to focus on thinking about how you will respond to questions about aspects of your work that you might struggle to explain clearly and comprehensively. It may be tempting to avoid thinking about these aspects, but it is guaranteed that these will be exactly the issues that your examiners will ask questions about. It is also worth spending time preparing a response to the commonly asked first question/request (Please summarise the aims, objectives, method/design and key findings of your study). Use the time between thesis submission and viva to revisit your reflective diary. While talking to friends and colleagues who have recently had their viva may be useful, remember that there is a risk of your being exposed to their viva horror stories. Therefore, be judicious about who you talk to and remember that no two vivas are ever exactly the same.

If you are required to give a presentation as part of your viva, ensure that this is prepared in good time. Rehearse the presentation with a volunteer audience to check the content, the format of the material used and the timing. All candidates should take a copy of their thesis into the viva. A copy in a ring binder is more accessible than a bound copy and do not put whole chapters into A4 plastic wallets because individual pages will be difficult to access quickly. It is worth spending time in the weeks before the viva to use post-it notes (or similar) to identify the chapters and any aspects of your thesis that you feel are particularly significant. However, do not be over elaborate. Developing a complicated colour-coded system may take a lot of time, and although it may look impressive, being unable to find the part of your thesis that you need during the viva may cause you to feel flustered.

The mock viva

The mock viva is the most common formal kind of viva preparation. In some institutions, the mock viva is optional, while for others it is compulsory. It is usually undertaken a couple of weeks before the actual viva and is conducted by academics from the institution where the doctorate was studied and may include the candidate's critical reader (see above). The mock viva examiners will have had access to the student's thesis, but rather than reading the whole document, they are often asked to read and ask questions about one or two chapters each. It is worth considering the pros and cons of having a mock viva.

Activity 8.3

What do you think are the pros and cons of doing a mock viva?

If conducted in a professional and supportive manner, the mock viva can be an invaluable practice run for the candidate, particularly for those who have not previously participated in this type of examination. The mock viva should be conducted following the likely format of the actual viva and under the same conditions, although it may be carried out without a Chair. A member of the supervisory team should attend if the student wishes. The mock viva examiners are usually asked to give feedback not only on the candidate's responses to the questions, but also on the way in which they conducted themselves. Mock examiner feedback can therefore be very helpful in highlighting issues that the candidate can focus on during their final weeks of viva preparation. However, we acknowledge that for some candidates the mock viva can be counterproductive. There is no way of knowing that the issues raised by the mock viva examiners will be the same as those raised by the actual examiners. It may also be too late to address issues that are raised in the mock viva. So rather than the identification of potentially problematic aspects of the thesis being helpful, it can become the focus of the candidate's worries and concerns in the run up to the actual viva. In extreme cases, particularly if the mock viva is conducted in an unprofessional or unsupportive way, it can have an adverse effect on the candidate's confidence.

The selection of academics to examine the mock viva is therefore crucial. The institution will probably have criteria on who can undertake this role. Your supervisory team and doctoral college will probably take the lead, but you may also be invited to express an opinion. At least one of the examiners should have a knowledge of the subject area and the methodology used. They should be known within the institution to be constructive, supportive and to be someone whose judgement you respect. For academics undertaking their doctorate in their home institution, the selection of mock viva examiners can be an added challenge. You may feel concerned that the process will leave you feeling exposed if the examiners are already known to you. It may therefore be worth considering the involvement of examiners who are less well known to you, perhaps from another faculty or department.

If you have a choice on whether or not to have a mock viva, you should consider how helpful it is likely to be to *you* and not be swayed by what other doctoral students usually do in your institution. In making your decision, think about how you generally respond to criticism.

Activity 8.4

What do you think are the pros and cons *for you* of doing a mock viva?

Following the mock viva, the student should meet with their supervisory team to 'debrief'. This will be particularly useful if a member of the supervisory team attended the mock viva. The supervisory team should work with the student to identify issues to focus on in the final weeks of viva preparation. This does not necessarily mean addressing the content of the thesis. Rather, the focus could be on having further practice at responding to questions about the study. If the mock viva has identified any serious flaws or concerns, the supervisory team should work with the student to develop a strategy on how these will be managed in the actual viva (see below). We offer two contrasting views of the mock viva in the case studies below.

Case study 8.4

Cora chose not to have a mock viva. She had a viva as part of her Master's assessment and also when attaining her professional qualification. In addition, she regularly conducted vivas with undergraduate students. Cora therefore felt comfortable with the process. Throughout her doctorate, she had close interactions with the small team of academics in the department of the institution where she was undertaking her doctorate. She was also required to present a summary of her doctorate to the team six months before she submitted her thesis. Cora therefore felt she had received the academics' feedback and support throughout her doctorate. Rather than having a mock viva, Cora worked with her supervisor to identify potential questions and her likely responses.

Case study 8.5

Tom opted to have a mock viva. As a lecturer, Tom was used to teaching both large and small groups. Nevertheless, he was nervous about the viva, but felt he should try to put on a 'brave face' in front of his mock examiners and supervisory team. In the early part of the mock viva, he stumbled over his responses and had to ask for several questions to be repeated. He also 'lost his way' in his answer to a more complex question and had to start his response again. However, the examiners were supportive and gave him the time to consider his responses. As the viva progressed, Tom became more confident and began to enjoy the event. He was surprised at how exhausted he felt afterwards. The examiners gave him detailed and helpful feedback, which primarily focused on his need to develop his verbal reasoning skills.

Appointing the right examiners

The institution will have regulations on how many doctorate examiners are required and who can undertake the role. There will probably be two or three examiners and an independent Chair, although in some institutions, the internal examiner will also be the Chair. The number of examiners may be determined by the doctorate examination experience of the proposed examiners. For example, if one of the potential examiners has limited experience, an additional examiner may be required. In most institutions, the doctoral college and supervisory team work together to identify potential examiners and secure their appointment.

At least one of the examiners should have a knowledge of the subject area and the methodology used. You may have had one or two examiners in mind for some time (see above). In some instances, a member of the supervisory team will approach potential examiners informally to 'sound them out'. We suggest that before any final decisions are made, it is essential to be clear about any agenda or stance that the examiners may have that could impact on the way in which the thesis is examined and the viva is conducted (see above). There can be a great deal of snobbery about the selection of doctorate examiners, with the view among some that they should have national, or indeed international, reputations. It is of course important that they are credible and we acknowledge that doctoral examiners may be useful in the longer term with networking, the provision of testimonies or collaborations. However, the person who is most well known in the field may not be the most appropriate examiner for you. Reputations (either positive or negative) may be inaccurate or unfairly assigned. Nevertheless, there will be some people who are known to be combative or to have an agenda that contrasts with the stance you have taken. They are best avoided and your supervisory team should advise you on this. For academics undertaking their doctorate in their home institution, the selection of the internal examiner can present additional challenges. Reputations will be more clearly known, although they can still be biased. You may feel concerned that the doctorate examination process will leave you feeling exposed if the examiner is already known to you. It can also be more difficult to find someone you have not worked with directly, particularly in smaller institutions or specialist subject areas. It may be worth considering the appointment of an internal examiner who is less well known to you, perhaps from a different faculty or department.

Once the examiners are agreed, the institution will have a formal process of appointment. This usually begins when the candidate has formally notified their institution of their 'intention to submit' or similar (see above). A central department of the institution or the doctoral college, rather than the candidate's supervisory team, usually organises the notification process. It can take several months for formal appointments to be agreed, so it is important to ensure that adequate time is allowed for this in your doctoral timeline.

Appointing the right chair

The Chair will be an academic from the institution where the doctorate has been undertaken. The institution will have regulations on who can undertake the role, including the stipulation that the person has had a specific amount of prior experience as a doctoral examiner. Often the Chair will also be required to have undertaken specific training before taking on the role. Consequently, many institutions will have a limited number of people they can draw upon. There may therefore be fewer options when it comes to appointing the Chair. Nevertheless, the person should be fair, supportive and respected. The Chair is often unknown to the candidate, although this is less likely for academics undertaking a doctorate in their home institution. Academics being examined within their own institution may therefore feel more comfortable if a chair from another faculty or department is appointed.

The viva itself

There is no getting away from the fact that for most people the doctoral viva is a daunting prospect (Knight et al., 2018). Indeed, to some extent it should be, as it is the culmination of many years of hard work and sacrifice, and candidate apprehension acknowledges its significance. It could be argued that candidates who do not feel nervous about their viva are probably either over-confident or naive. Nevertheless, anxiety can become counterproductive for some and so it is worth considering strategies that you can put in place to keep your nervousness under control. You will know what works best for you. Doing something the evening before, such as going to the cinema, the gym or spending time with friends and family, may work for you. Alternatively, you might prefer a quiet evening at home. While reading through aspects of your thesis in the days before your viva is recommended, doing so the evening or night before the viva may unsettle rather than calm you.

Reflection 8.1

What works best for you to calm exam nerves?

Give some thought to what you will wear on the day. You should be smart, but it is more important to be comfortable. As we discussed earlier, you should take a copy of your thesis into the viva. Ideally, a member of your supervisory team or the doctoral college will take you into the viva, even if they do not stay. If you are going to the viva on your own, ensure that you know exactly where it is taking place. Do not assume that you will be able to find the venue on the day. If the viva is being held in an unfamiliar room or location, make sure that you can find it beforehand.

As you go into the room, remember that you know more about your study than anyone else. Be proud of your work and what you have achieved. However nervous you are feeling, giving a cheerful 'hello' as you enter the room will help to calm your nerves. The panel should welcome you and invite you to sit down. Do not be afraid to take a bit of time to ensure that you feel comfortable, or as comfortable as you can be under the circumstances! The viva usually begins with the examiners introducing themselves, including those you already know. Do not be over-familiar, particularly with examiners already known to you. If you are required to give a presentation, ensure that you are happy with the IT equipment before you start. Ask the Chair for help rather than struggle on your own.

While guides and resources are available regarding common viva questions (see the book's online resources), it will commonly begin and end with straightforward questions that you should be comfortable about answering. The more searching and probing questions will probably occur in the middle of the viva. Sometimes examiners will put candidates at their ease at the start of the viva by making a complimentary statement about the thesis. However, if this comment is not forthcoming, do not make negative assumptions. It may be that making such a comment is not part of the examiners' usual practice.

The viva will often begin with something along the lines of 'Please summarise the aims, objectives, method/design and key findings of your study'. Sometimes this is referred to as asking you to present the 'five-minute thesis'. Alternatively, you may be asked 'What does your study add to the current body of knowledge?'. You should plan for these types of question, bearing in mind that what you prepare may need to be adjusted to ensure it addresses the specific question or request. Therefore, while learning a script verbatim beforehand may be tempting and comforting, it can confuse both you and the examiners if what you have prepared does not exactly match what they have asked. Try to give the requested information in a succinct way. You may be asked to summarise more briefly if it becomes apparent that you are giving an overly lengthy answer and you may find this disconcerting. Do not assume that the examiners have a hidden agenda if they ask questions that appear straightforward or require simple answers. They may be attempting to put you at ease, or they may just require some clarification. If you feel that referring the examiners to a specific part of your thesis (such as a diagram or data table) will facilitate your response, then direct them to it at the beginning of your answer. This will give you a bit of time to compose your answer and will show that you are able to apply your answer to key aspects of your work.

Try to adopt a relaxed but professional posture during the viva. Maintain eye contact with the examiners if you can, although we acknowledge that this may not be appropriate in some cultures. Some tips about responding to questions, which are based on our experiences over time, are as follows:

- Answer the question that has been asked. Do not be tempted to throw in erroneous information.
- Sometimes examiners will ask questions that appear to challenge the decisions that you have made. Do not assume, in the first instance, that they think that what you did was inappropriate. They probably want to ensure that you can give a clear rationale for your decisions.
- If asked a question that you do not understand, ask the examiner to repeat or rephrase it.
- Do not be afraid to pause and think about your answer before you jump in with your response.
- If you feel you need more time to consider your response, then say, 'May I just think about that?' and collate your thoughts.
- If you become aware that your answer is starting to deviate away from the question, acknowledge this and refocus your response.
- If during your response, you lose track of the original question, then acknowledge this and ask the examiner(s) to repeat the question.
- If you are asked a question that you cannot answer, acknowledge this rather than vacillating or answering a question they have not asked.
- If the examiners point out something that you have not considered, then acknowledge this.
- Do not directly blame your supervisors during the viva for any inability on your part to answer a question, although you could couch this more generally along the lines of, 'This is not something that we have considered'.
- If the examiners identify a flaw that you are already aware of (for example, something identified during the mock viva), then acknowledge this by saying that you and your supervisory team identified the error after submission. Be proactive and indicate what you plan to do in order to put it right.

Most vivas run for one to two hours. If partway through you feel that you need a break, then ask for one. The Chair in particular should be sensitive to a candidate's need for a break, but if the offer is not forthcoming, then do not be afraid to ask. The closing questions of the viva usually focus on your professional development during the doctorate, your plans for the dissemination of the work or potential post-doctoral work. Sometimes examiners are interested to hear about the level of support you have received during your doctorate. You should think in advance about your likely responses to these types of question. However, these should be issues that you feel comfortable talking about spontaneously. Usually, the viva ends with your being asked if there is anything that you wish to add. Try to say something at this point. For example, you may feel that there is an important aspect of your work that has not been covered or you may wish to acknowledge the support you have received. You may also wish to acknowledge that you have noted since the submission of your thesis, spelling or referencing errors that need to be corrected. When the viva is over, you will be asked to leave the room. Try to remember to thank the examiners. You will probably be asked to wait somewhere nearby so that you can be called back into the room to be told the outcome. If at all possible, either a member of your supervisory team or the doctoral college or a friend or colleague should wait with you. However, you may prefer to be alone at this time and that is fine if it is what you want.

It is not uncommon for a candidate to have a release of emotion on leaving the viva. You are not being weak or feeble if you shed a tear. Try not to overthink what has just happened and instead have some quiet downtime. Remember that the length of the viva does not necessarily indicate the likely outcome. Lots of questions or a lengthy viva do not necessarily mean that there are lots of problems with your work. It is more likely that the examiners enjoyed reading your thesis and were genuinely interested to talk with you about it. Often when the viva is over, candidates acknowledge that it was a more enjoyable experience than they had anticipated (Davis and Engward, 2018). At its best, a viva should feel more like a conversation with the examiners rather than feeling that you have been 'on trial'.

The length of time that you have to wait before being called back to meet the examiners is not necessarily indicative of the outcome. Remember that, like you, the examiners will almost certainly need a comfort break and some refreshments. They will also have to agree and collate their feedback and reach a decision about the outcome. The Chair will oversee this process to ensure that the institution's regulations are followed.

You will, in the fullness of time, be called back into the room. Again, a member of your supervisory team may accompany you if you wish. You will be told the outcome, whether any amendments are required and, if so, the required timescale in which you need to make the corrections. This may all pass in a blur and you will probably only remember the overall outcome decision. If a member of your supervisory team is with you, they should take notes about any required amendments and the timescale you have to make the changes. You will ultimately receive a letter from the doctoral college detailing the decision and any amendments that are required. However, this may take a week or so to arrive, so your supervisor's notes may be helpful in the interim. Try to remember to thank the examiners as you leave the room.

Some institutions arrange a post-viva tea party or celebratory drink for the candidate. Only you will know if this is something that you are likely to want. However, in most cases, candidates are exhausted after their viva and prefer to take themselves away from the setting and have some 'down time' with family or friends or on their own. Whatever you decide, the key thing to tell yourself is that having your viva is an important milestone in your doctoral journey.

Within this chapter we have explored the final stages of your doctoral journey: preparing for the submission of your thesis and your viva. In the following chapter we will review the different categories of doctoral outcome and strategies to help you to deal with these. We also conclude the book by considering life beyond the doctorate and offer suggestions about how to let go of your doctorate and build on your doctoral life.

To access the online resources accompanying this chapter, please visit:
https://study.sagepub.com/harvey

Nine

Arriving at your destination

In this final chapter we discuss the different potential outcomes of your thesis and viva and explore some strategies to support you in making any required amendments. In doing this, we acknowledge that a requirement to revise and resubmit a thesis and/ or undertake a second viva can be especially difficult for an academic undertaking their doctorate in their home institution. We conclude the chapter, and indeed this book, by considering life beyond the doctorate, offering suggestions about how to move on. This includes 'letting go' of your doctoral life and making plans for your continued professional development and career progression.

As was the case in previous chapters, case studies are used as illustrations. We have also included short reflective pieces from academics who have recently completed their doctorate. Throughout the chapter, you will be directed to a range of tools and resources for ongoing support that can be found on the book's accompanying online resources.

Potential doctoral examination outcomes

Having submitted your thesis for examination and undertaken your viva, there are a range of potential examination outcomes that you may be awarded. The wording and criteria of these different outcomes can vary between institutions. You should therefore check your institution's examination outcome options. However, in principle, they will be:

- Award outright
- Award subject to amendments to be made over a short time period or to minor amendments
- Award subject to amendments to be made over a longer time period or to major amendments
- Requirement to resubmit the thesis (which may include having a second viva)
- Award lower degree (possibly following previous resubmission)
- Withdraw with no right to resubmit.

Some of these potential outcomes may seem alarming. However, what you should remember is that your supervisors and doctoral college will strongly advise you not to submit if they feel you are at risk of the latter two outcomes. Similarly, the progression points that you will have been required to pass during your doctorate should preclude either of these outcomes occurring. Nevertheless, some students for a variety of reasons choose to submit against their supervisors' or doctoral college's advice. Alternatively, some students run out of time and may have to submit even if they and their supervisory team are aware that the thesis is not as developed as they would like it to be. We will therefore review all potential outcomes in this section.

Award outright

This is a relatively rare outcome. It means that both the viva and thesis have met the required standard for this award. However, in almost all cases the thesis will require some form of amendment. Some institutions will award a doctorate outright on the understanding that a very small number of amendments are required. This may amount to correcting one or two spelling errors, for example. The candidate will almost certainly be able to use the title 'Doctor' straight away and the award will be confirmed at the next available Examination Board.

Award subject to amendments to be made over a short time period or to minor amendments

This is a more common outcome. It means that the viva has been passed but that amendments are needed to the thesis. Sometimes amendments are deemed to be 'minor', although definitions of 'minor' can vary according to the institution. Minor amendments can include the correction of errors in spelling, referencing and grammar, making amendments to the format of some of the tables, graphs and charts, amending cross-referencing or the repositioning of content. Minor amendments do not usually require new material to be added beyond sentences to link content or additional brief explanatory information. The required changes will be detailed in a letter from the doctoral college which is sent to the candidate and their supervisory team following the viva. The timeframe to make these amendments is usually three to six months. However, part-time students are often given longer, particularly if they are working full-time at this point. The examiners will agree which one of them will 'sign off' the amendments. This is usually the internal examiner. The institution will advise the candidate whether they can use the title 'Doctor' immediately. It is usually the case that they can. Once the amendments have been approved, the award will be confirmed at the next available Examination Board.

Award subject to amendments to be made over a longer time period or to major amendments

This outcome is more common than perhaps most doctoral students would like. This means that the viva has been passed but that more extensive amendments need to be made to the thesis. 'Major' amendments usually necessitate the changes required for 'minor' amendments and the inclusion of new content. The required changes will be detailed in a letter from the doctoral college which is sent to the candidate and their supervisory team following the viva. The examiners will agree which one of them will 'sign off' the amendments. This may be the internal examiner, but often it is decided that all the examiners should review the amended thesis. The timeframe to make these amendments is usually six to 12 months. Part-time students are often given a minimum of 12 months, particularly if they are working full-time at this point. The institution will advise the candidate whether they can use the title 'Doctor' immediately; it is often the case that they can. Once the amendments have been approved, the award will be confirmed at the next available Examination Board.

There is no shame in being asked to make major amendments to your thesis. Nevertheless, the term 'major' can imply to some that the required changes are considerable and that this in turn has negative connotations regarding the quality of the original work. As a consequence, some institutions have stopped using the terms 'minor' and 'major' and instead use the timeframe allocated to make the required changes as a means of distinguishing between the two.

Case study 9.1

Although Alfredia successfully passed her viva, she was initially disappointed to be given a year to amend her thesis. She had previously secured a six-month sabbatical to write up her thesis and had used the time wisely. Alfredia now felt embarrassed that her thesis required further work and was frustrated that her supervisory team had let her submit work that required further attention. Alfredia and her supervisory team reviewed the required amendments and she then realised that they were not as extensive as she had assumed. Her supervisory team felt sure Alfredia had been given a year to make the amendments out of recognition of her extensive workload.

Requirement to resubmit the thesis

This outcome is given when further research and/or a rewrite of the thesis is required. A second viva may be needed, at the discretion of the examiners. The decision about the viva may not be made until the examiners have reviewed the resubmitted thesis. While a resubmission outcome might be disappointing, the doctorate is usually subsequently awarded. The required changes will be detailed in a letter from the doctoral college which is sent to the candidate and their supervisory team following the viva. The timeframe to resubmit the thesis is usually 12 months. Candidates who find themselves in this situation should establish whether they will be required to pay additional fees. Academics undertaking their doctorate in their home institution should not assume that any additional fees will be covered by their employer (see below).

Award lower degree

Depending on the institution's regulations, it is extremely rare for this to be the outcome decision following the first submission of a doctoral thesis and the viva.

However, it may be an option for the examiners after the resubmission of a doctoral thesis and repeat viva. A lower degree is awarded if the candidate is deemed not to meet the requirements of the doctorate. The lower degree that an institution awards will vary, but it will usually be an MPhil, MSc or MA. Some further amendments may be required to the resubmitted thesis before this award can be made.

Withdraw with no right to resubmit

This is an extremely unlikely outcome, which is reserved for a resubmitted doctoral thesis and repeat viva that are deemed not to meet the requirements of a lower degree. We strongly believe that supervisory teams and doctoral colleges have a responsibility to ensure that students do not find themselves in this situation. Strategies should be in place to prevent this scenario occurring. The one situation where it may occur is if the candidate has chosen not to follow guidance and advice. Nevertheless, the student may ultimately have a case to pursue a claim for 'material error' if they feel that the institution has not followed required procedures.

Making amendments: The practicalities

Following the post-viva euphoria, and in many cases the award of doctorate subject to amendments, the reality is that the changes have to be made within the required timeframe. While it might be tempting to 'jump straight in' and make the changes, a period of time away from the doctorate is often recommended because this will enable you to come back to it with a fresh pair of eyes and renewed energy. You will know if this strategy is likely to be of benefit to you. To some extent the decision to make amendments straight away will be determined by the nature and extent of any forth-coming commitments you may have, both professional and personal.

Irrespective of your thoughts, or those of your supervisory team, about the requested amendments, they need to be followed to the letter. The examiner reviewing your revised thesis will check it against the list of required amendments. If something remains outstanding, you will be asked to revise your thesis again. You should there-fore work through the required amendments with your supervisory team to ensure that they have all been addressed before you submit the revised copy. If a member of your supervisory team attended your viva, their notes will be a useful resource. Most institutions require candidates to present their amendments in a specific for-mat. For example, it may include submitting two copies of your thesis: one clean copy with the amendments made and one copy with the amendments highlighted. Alternatively, you may be required to submit a letter with your thesis in which you list the required changes along with the page number where each amendment can be found. You should always follow the institution's required format. If the institution does not provide guidance on this, we advise that you work with your supervisory team to develop a system that will enable the examiner(s) to locate the amendments easily (see the online resources for an example). Having a systematic approach will help you to ensure that all of the required changes have been made. It will also break down the required changes into more manageable tasks. Some institutions advocate asking another academic, who has had no prior involvement with the student's doctorate, to check that all the required amendments have been made before the thesis is resubmitted. Again, if your institution does not adopt such a procedure, it may be worth asking a colleague to do this for you. Remember, that the amended work will need proof-reading before it is resubmitted. Proof-reading should include checking that section headings, numbering and the table of contents remain correct and any new references have been inserted correctly.

It is absolutely essential that a realistic timeframe is identified to complete the amendments, especially for those undertaking their doctorate on a part-time basis. As identified earlier, it may be tempting to rush to get the amendments made. However, it is safer to allocate longer than should be required to cover unexpected eventualities. For academics, the allocation of further study time will almost certainly mean that aspects of their workload will need to be renegotiated. You should therefore discuss the allocation of study time with your line manager at the earliest opportunity. In some institutions, candidates may be required to pay additional fees while they make their amendments and you should establish if this will be the case for you.

Making amendments: The impact on you

There is no doubt that having to make changes to your thesis can be disappointing, for you, your supervisory team, family, friends and colleagues. However, having to make amendments does not mean that you are a failure. Instead, they are ways in which your work can be enhanced and, in turn, be more valuable to readers of your work in the future.

Submitting the thesis and participating in the viva may have seemed beforehand to be the likely end point of your doctorate. However, for some students another year (or more) is required in order to be awarded their doctorate. In some instances, there may have been a lack of understanding, naivety or over-confidence about the overall timeframe or the quality of the work. Nevertheless, time to make possible amendments should be factored into the overall doctorate timeline. In the light of the possibility of having to make amendments, it is sensible for a student not to plan anything that may compromise their availability to make their amendments in the time required. For example, it may be prudent not to book six months' international travel immediately post-viva.

Do not be disappointed if you have been given a year to make your amendments. As we have identified earlier, this does not necessarily mean that major amendments are required or that the quality of your original work was of concern. It may simply be that your examiners have acknowledged that you now have a full workload and feel that you should be given a longer period of time in which to make the necessary amendments.

Maintaining momentum and motivation while making the required changes can be a challenge in the same ways that we discussed in Chapter 5. What you need to remember is that you have come such a long way. To not complete now would be a waste of time, money, effort, sacrifice and the support you have received along the way. You also have a duty to the research participants to complete your work. Consequently, you will need to find a way of working that suits you best. Developing an action plan with the required tasks identified in manageable pieces may be helpful. It may be tempting to complete the changes as quickly as you can. However, you should not risk compromising the quality of your revisions. As we have already identified, if the required changes are not to the satisfaction of the examiners, you will only be asked to amend your work again. Rather than jumping straight in, you may prefer to give yourself a short break so that you can come back to the amendments feeling re-energised. However, if you know that this strategy is likely to cause you to feel less rather than more focused, then it is probably best avoided.

For academics undertaking a doctorate in their home institution, a requirement to revise and resubmit a thesis and/or to undertake a second viva can be especially difficult. In this situation, they cannot simply 'disappear' during this time. In addition, workloads may have already been set based on an assumption of the doctorate completion date. Having to renegotiate workloads may be difficult and requires sensitivity from all concerned. We recommend that you work with your supervisory team to establish exactly how long it is likely to take you to make the amendments, irrespective of the time you have been allocated by the examiners. You need to be honest about the total amount of time required and whether it would be better for you to take any allocated study time incrementally or to amalgamate it into blocks of time. You then need to inform your line manager and map out a plan, as it may also require a negotiation with colleagues to reallocate workloads. It is fair to say that some line managers may be unsupportive to any request for additional study time as they may feel you have already had your share. Your doctoral college and supervisory team may be able to advise you about what you may be entitled to and strategies you can adopt to pursue a reasonable allocation of study time. We would strongly argue that it will be in both your institution's and immediate team's best interests for you to successfully complete your doctorate, not least in terms of successful doctorate completions for the Research Exercise Framework (REF, 2019) and for the institution to secure a reputation of being a supportive working environment. As part of your discussion about your support post-viva, you may need to establish if additional fees are required. This will be determined by the institution's regulations and you should not assume that these will be covered by your employer.

Resubmitting your amendments

Institutions vary in their procedures regarding the resubmission of amendments. You should therefore be advised by your supervisory team and doctoral college about what you should do. While examiners will aim to review your amendments as punctually as they can, you must remember that they will inevitably have other commitments. Most doctoral colleges request that examiner reports are required within six to ten weeks. However, some institutions do not give examiners a required timeframe.

If a repeat viva is needed, our guidance in Chapter 8 applies regarding viva preparation. In addition, the candidate and supervisory team should take note of any feedback from the examiners regarding the first viva. This will facilitate strategies being put in place to prepare the student for the second viva, and may include undertaking a practice viva and or going on a course or workshop on verbal reasoning.

Waiting for the outcome following the submission of amendments and a repeat viva can be especially difficult. You may feel by this time that you have had more than enough of your doctorate! You may also find it difficult to handle constantly being asked by friends, family and colleagues when you will hear the outcome. Remember that they ask because they care about you and have been interested in your doctoral journey. It is likely that your overwhelming feeling on hearing that your amendments have been accepted and your doctorate awarded will be that of relief.

Life post-doctorate

In the final section of the book we focus on life post-doctorate for the academic who has undertaken their doctorate either in their home or an external institution, although we anticipate that much of our discussion will be applicable to other doctoral students in other contexts.

First, many congratulations! You have secured your doctorate. You should take some time to bask in the glory of what you have achieved. Your supervisory team, family, friends and colleagues will be justifiably proud of what you have accomplished. You may not feel comfortable about having a large celebration, but it is important that your achievement is recognised. Sometimes you have to let those who have supported you celebrate. To some extent, if they have invested time and effort supporting you, this is also their success.

Moving forwards, on a purely practical note, ensure that your curriculum vitae is updated, along with any documentation regarding your performance review. Make sure that any other professional documentation about you is also amended. This may include information on websites, in journals, in any in-house directories and your email signature.

Remember that you are now a role model for other academics who might be considering undertaking a doctorate or who are partway through one. You will probably quite quickly be asked to provide advice, guidance or support, if not to take on the more formal role of supervisor (which is discussed below). You may feel that you have hardly had time to draw breath and it can be quite daunting to feel that you are now considered to be the 'expert' in studying for a doctorate. For all doctoral students it is important that their work is disseminated in papers and conference presentations, as appropriate (see below). However, what happens for you now professionally depends to some extent on your original reason(s) for doing a doctorate (see Chapter 2).

Reflection 9.1

Revisit your original reasons for doing a doctorate. Have you added any other reasons along the way?

Irrespective of the opportunities currently available within your institution, what would you like to do professionally now that you have attained your doctorate?

Some people are more than happy to return to or continue with their roles and responsibilities. This is absolutely fine, if it is what you want. However, for many, doing a doctorate gives them a taste of what they may be able to achieve in the future in order to fully utilise the skills and knowledge they have developed. Your professional life post-doctorate will probably depend on your discipline and the opportunities within your current institution. However, do not let your future working life be shaped by a lack of opportunity. This may be the time for a change of role within your institution. Alternatively, you may decide to seek employment elsewhere.

In your current institution, you may be able to negotiate refocusing aspects of your current role and responsibilities or you may choose to apply for a different post within the organisation. Rightly or wrongly, before any change in role can occur you may first have to 'prove your worth'. It may include publishing aspects of your doctorate, presenting your work at conferences, participating in teaching research (if you do not do this already) or securing research funding. There may be other things you can do, such as setting up a doctoral forum for academics currently undertaking a doctorate (see Chapter 7).

Activity 9.1

Based on your doctoral experiences, write a piece for current or prospective doctoral students in which you offer advice that you wished you had been given at the start of your doctorate. Try to give keep it positive and constructive.

For some who have achieved a doctorate, it may be possible for them to move immediately to undertaking post-doctoral research. To some extent this will depend on the discipline and availability of funding opportunities. It is perhaps less likely that academics will have opportunities for post-doctoral work. Rather, there is more likely to be the expectation within the organisation that they will return to, or continue, their former role with the associated workloads. Nevertheless, if post-doctoral research is something you would like to pursue, you should discuss it with your line manager and those with faculty or institutional responsibility for research. It would also be worth exploring potential funding opportunities.

Disseminating your doctorate findings

Sadly, the findings from doctoral studies are not always disseminated. There may be a variety of reasons for this, and for academics resuming a full workload finding time for dissemination can be problematic (Broadhurst, 2014). However, researchers have a responsibility to both the study participants and their funder to share their findings. Publication in peer-review journals and evaluation of impact are also becoming increasingly important to academic institutions (REF, 2019).

Getting published

Successful students should endeavour in the early months post-doctorate to pursue publication of their work. This is the time when your study will be most fresh in your mind and working on publications may be a good way of winding down from your doctorate. Think of publication as completing the doctoral circle. Negotiate with your line manager to secure time to work on publications and ensure that this goal is included in your performance review.

Depending on the subject area and discipline, it may be more appropriate to publish a book rather than several papers. Having one or more co-authors can help to maintain your motivation. In addition, co-authoring with experienced academics can be a supportive experience for those with limited or no publication experience (Broadhurst, 2014). Most commonly, co-authors might be found in your supervisory team but, depending on the subject area, it may also be appropriate to work alongside colleagues who have recently completed their doctorate.

─── Case study 9.2 ──────────────────────────────────

Harriet and Keith are lecturers who undertook their part-time doctorates at the same time, but at different institutions. They had known each other for many years and were members of the same professional organisation. Their doctorates were in the same broad subject area but they pursued completely different studies, using different methodologies and studying different populations. On completion of their doctorates, they realised that they could combine their literature reviews, which ultimately resulted in a book that was published two years later.

Most supervisors will readily agree to work with former doctoral students on papers for publication. From the outset, you should agree authorship and the extent to which your supervisory team will be involved. It should be noted that securing publication in peer-review journals is becoming more challenging, particularly in the period immediately prior to a Research Exercise Framework (REF). Covering the cost of publishing in open-access publications, which is particularly desired by some disciplines, can also be problematic. You should therefore explore potential funding opportunities within your institution before opting for an open-access journal as an outlet for your work. Dealing with the rejection of papers and book proposals can be difficult, and it can be tempting to give up after the first unsuccessful attempt. However, you should have confidence in your work and not be deterred at the first hurdle. Seeing your work in print is a great morale boost and can open doors for you in the future. For example, it may help you to secure funding for post-doctoral work, a promotion or it may facilitate networking (Becker and Denicolo, 2012; Bolton and Rowland, 2014).

Activity 9.2

- Think about your recently completed doctorate and make a list of the different papers that you could develop from your work and identify potential publications for each.
- Identify aspects of your experiences of doing a doctorate that could be developed into papers for publication and identify potential publications for each.
- Identify potential co-authors for the papers you have listed.

Presenting your doctorate

The expectation that doctoral findings are presented at conferences is more established in some disciplines than others. To some extent it will depend on the availability of such conferences (both nationally and internationally) and the funding within your institution to support conference attendance. The latter may be an issue if there is a perception within your organisation that you have already had your share of funding as a consequence of doing your doctorate. If this is the case, you may be able to apply for bursaries or travel scholarships to support your attendance at conferences. Presenting at conferences can be a positive experience and an effective way of disseminating your findings and networking. The latter may, in turn, lead to further professional develop-ment or post-doctoral research opportunities. Generating a paper for conference pres-entation can also act as a precursor to developing papers for publication. For example, the structure of a presentation can form the basis of a future paper.

Although as an academic you will be familiar with teaching and presenting, the thought of presenting your own work can be daunting. Putting your hard work of the last few years 'out there' for the direct scrutiny of an audience can feel exposing. However, you should feel confident in your work. You have been awarded a doctor-ate and that in itself is a measure of the depth, breadth and quality of your work. Some academics will be more familiar with presenting work at national and inter-national conferences than others. To build up your confidence, you could start with in-house presentations at internal conferences, meetings or research groups. A range of resources are available to support those who are less experienced at presenting at conferences (Becker, 2014; Nygaard, 2015).

Case study 9.3

Although an experienced lecturer, Peter has never presented at an external conference. He identified in his annual performance review that he would like to do this and his line manager was supportive. They agreed that, in the first instance, Peter would present his doctorate findings at the bi-monthly team meeting.

Activity 9.3

Think about your recently completed doctorate and make a list of the different conference papers that you could develop from your work. Identify potential external conferences and in-house events where you could present each paper.

Identify aspects of your experiences of doing a doctorate that could be developed into conference papers. Identify potential external conferences and in-house events where you could present each paper.

Becoming a supervisor

Becoming a doctorate supervisor can be quite daunting, but you are perfectly qualified to do it as you have had the most recent experience of being a doctoral student and know all that goes with it. In terms of supervising doctoral students, your institution may want you to take some time post-doctorate, say six months, before you start to do this. However, we strongly advocate that you begin supervising doctoral candidates as soon as you can in order to share your experiences. It will also be a professional development opportunity for you. Ideally, you should start slowly, with one or two students, and you should work alongside an experienced supervisor. Your doctoral college will probably deliver in-house supervisor training and we urge you to undertake whatever training is available.

If taking on a supervisory role feels too scary, perhaps the role of a mentor or 'buddy' could be a first step. Supporting doctoral students who have reached specific time points (such as progression assessment or their viva) may also be something you could handle. If your institution runs a doctoral forum, you could perhaps get involved with that. Do not underestimate what you can offer to current doctoral students.

Case study 9.4

It was made very clear to Zöe that, having completed her doctorate, her home institution expected her to take on the role of supervisor at the earliest opportunity. She discovered that she had automatically been scheduled to attend the in-house supervisor training programme. Zöe's first supervisory experience was working alongside one of her former supervisors. At first, she found this rather strange but quickly began to enjoy the experience. She found that she was able to provide her supervisee with practical guidance and support. She also felt that this new perspective of doctoral supervision was a tremendous learning opportunity for her.

Letting go of your doctorate

Probably the most challenging aspect of post-doctorate life is 'letting go' of it. Although this will be something you have longed for over several years, it can nevertheless feel strange and as if you have a vacuum to fill. Your doctorate will have given you a structure and purpose and your professional life can suddenly feel empty. Returning to work with a full workload can also be a shock to the system. Despite having to juggle your workload during your doctorate, you may have been shielded against some aspects of academic life. Feeling the full force of it once more, especially when you are probably still feeling drained by your doctoral experiences, can be difficult. It can also be frustrating to find that some aspects of academic life have not moved on and, conversely, that getting 'up to speed' with changes can be daunting. Seeing others having study time while they pursue their doctorate can be challenging, particularly if you feel they are receiving more support than you did. However, be assured that any current vacuum will soon be filled. Take control of the situation and use any gaps to write for publication or to prepare conference presentations. If you don't fill the gaps, you can be certain that someone else will. However, gaps should not only be filled with work-related or professional activities. There may be aspects of your life that you have 'put on hold' in recent years, and now is the time to return to those activities in order to re-establish a work–personal life balance.

Activity 9.4

Make a commitment to yourself now. Having successfully completed your doctorate, identify activities that you will return to or take up, or treats that you will reward yourself with.

The key thing is to be proactive and to take up activities, roles and responsibilities that you want to do, rather than those that others think you should do. You should feel in control of your professional roles and responsibilities. Use your doctorate as a platform to advocate for yourself. In doing this, you will be setting a trail for others to follow.

Our aim in writing this book was to create a resource to guide academics undertaking a part-time doctorate in their home institution. Our motivation for doing this was the recognition that the specific needs and the particular challenges encountered by this group have, to date, generally been neglected in the literature. In this book, we have not shied away from the challenges and negative elements that academics face. However, we hope that it will equip you with the skills and confidence to navigate your doctoral journey to its successful completion.

To access the online resources accompanying this chapter, please visit:
https://study.sagepub.com/harvey

References

Anderson, L.W., Krathwohl, D.R., Airasian, P.W., Cruikshank, K.A., Mayer, R.E., Pintrich, P.R., Raths, J. and Wittrock, M.C. (2001) *A Taxonomy for Learning, Teaching and Assessing: A Revision of Bloom's Taxonomy of Educational Objectives.* New York: Longman.

Beattie, M. (2016) *A Reflection on Completing a PhD by Publication: The Learning Process* . Available at: https://researchandinnovationblog.stir.ac.uk/2016/10/31/a-reflection-on-completing-a-phd-by-publication-the-learning-process-by-michelle-beattie/ (accessed 15 September 2020).

Becker, L. (2014) *Presenting your research.* London: Sage.

Becker, L. and Denicolo, P. (2012) *Publishing Journal Articles.* London: Sage.

Birks, M. and Watson, R. (2018) Doctoral snobbery: Justified, or just elitism? *Journal of Advanced Nursing,* 74: 493–494.

Boliver, V. (2015) Are there distinctive clusters of higher and lower status universities in the UK? *Oxford Review of Education,* 41(5): 608–627.

Bolton, G. and Rowland, S. (2014) *Inspirational Writing for Academic Publication.* London: Sage.

Boncori, I. and Smith, C. (2020) Negotiating the doctorate as an academic professional: Identity work and sensemaking through authoethnographic methods. *Teaching in Higher Education,* 25(3): 271–285.

Bothello, J. and Roulet, T.J. (2019) The Imposter Syndrome, or the mis-representation of self in academic life. *Journal of Management Studies,* 56(4): 854–861.

Broadhurst, K. (2014) Academic publishing and the doctoral student: Lessons from Sweden. *Qualitative Social Work,* 13(5): 595–601.

Clark, A. and Sousa, B. (2018) *How to Be a Happy Academic.* London: Sage.

Cottrell, S. (2019) *The Study Skills Handbook.* London: Red Globe Press.

Davis, G. and Engward, H. (2018) In defence of the viva voce: Eighteen candidates' voices. *Nurse Education Today,* 65: 30–35.

Department of Education (2016) *A Teaching Excellence and Student Outcomes Framework.* Available at: https://www.gov.uk/government/collections/teaching-excellence-framework (accessed 10 November 2019).

Fillery-Travis, A. and Robinson, L. (2018) Making the familiar strange – a research pedagogy for practice. *Studies in Higher Education*, 43(5): 841–853.

Goodall, H.J., Huggins, V.A., Webber, L.A. and Wickett, K.L. (2017) From student to graduate: Four learners' perspectives of the professional doctorate journey. *Management in Education*, 31(4): 180–186.

Gray, M.A. and Crosta, L. (2019) New perspectives in online doctoral supervision: A systematic literature review. *Studies in Continuing Education*, 41(2): 173–190.

Guthrie, S., Litchen, C., van Belle, J., Ball, S., Knack, A. and Hofman, J. (2017) *Understanding Mental Health in the Research Environment: A Rapid Evidence Assessment*. Santa Monica, CA: RAND Corporation.

Harvey, M.E. and Land, L. (2017) *Research Methods for Nurses and Midwives*. London: Sage.

Hawkins, B. and Edwards, G. (2015) Managing the monsters of doubt: Liminality, threshold concepts and leadership learning. *Management Learning*, 46(1): 24–43.

Hay, A. and Samra-Fredericks, D. (2016) Desperately seeking fixedness: Practitioners' accounts of 'becoming doctoral researchers'. *Management Learning*, 47(4): 407–423.

Higher Education Funding Council for England (2009) *Outcomes Research Excellence Framework: Second Consultation on the Assessment and Funding of Research*. London: Higher Education Funding Council for England. Available at: https://webarchive.nationalarchives.gov.uk/20120314172944/http://www.hefce.ac.uk/pubs/consult/outcomes/ref2.asp (accessed 2 December 2019).

Higher Education Statistics Agency (2018) *Higher Education Qualifications Obtained by Level of Qualification*. Available at: www.hesa.ac.uk/news/11-01-2018/sfr247-higher-education-student-statistics/qualifications (accessed 13 February 2020).

Higher Education Student Statistics (HESA) (2020) *HE Student Enrolment by Level of Study*. Available at: https://www.hesa.ac.uk/news/16-01-2020/sb255-higher-education-student-statistics/numbers (accessed 17 January 2020).

Hill, M. (2002) Network assessments and diagrams. *Journal of Social Work*, 2(2): 233–254.

Hodgson, D. (2020) Helping doctoral students understand PhD thesis examination expectations: A framework and a tool for supervision. *Active Learning in Higher Education*, 21(1): 61–63.

Horta, H., Cattaneo, M. and Meolic, M. (2018) PhD funding as a determinant of PhD and career research performance. *Studies in Higher Education*, 43(3): 542–570.

Jackson, D. (2013) Completing a PhD by publication: A review of Australian policy and implications for practice. *Higher Education Research and Development*, 32(3): 355–368.

Jasper, M. (2006) *Professional Development, Reflection and Decision Making*. Oxford: Blackwell Publishing.

Knight, R.-A. Dipper, L. and Cruice, M. (2018) Viva survivors – the effect of peer-mentoring on pre-viva anxiety in early-years students. *Studies in Higher Education*, 43(1): 190–199.

Kornuta, H.M. and Germaine, R.W. (2019) *A Concise Guide to Writing a Thesis or Dissertation: Educational Research and Beyond* (2nd edition). Abingdon, UK: Routledge.

Kumar, S., Kumar, V. and Taylor, S. (2020) *A Guide to Online Supervision*. UK Council for Graduate Education. Available at: https://supervision.ukcge.ac.uk/cms/wp-content/uploads/A-Guideto-Online-Supervision-Kumar-Kumar-Taylor-UK-Council-for-Graduate-Education.pdf (accessed 4 September 2020).

Lee, G., Clark, A.M. and Thompson, D.R. (2012) Roses and thorns: Authorship and the PhD by publication. Commentary on Cleary, M., Jackson, D., Walter, G., Watson, R. & Hunt, G.F. (2012) Editorial: location, location, location – the position of authors in scholarly publishing. *Journal of Clinical Nursing*, 21: 809–811. *Journal of Clinical Nursing*, 22: 299–300.

Mantai, L. (2017) Feeling like a researcher: Experiences of early doctoral students in Australia. *Studies in Higher Education*, 42(4): 636–650.

Metcalf, J., Wilson, S. and Levecque, K. (2018) *Exploring Wellbeing and Mental Health and Associated Support Services for Postgraduate Researchers*. Cambridge: VITAE The Careers Research and Advisory Centre (CRAC) Limited.

Miller, G.A. (1957) The magical number seven, plus or minus two: Some limits on our capacity for processing information. *Psychological Review*, 63: 81–97.

Mills, S., Trehan, K. and Stewart, J. (2014) Academics in pursuit of the part-time doctorate: Pressures and support issues associated with the career development of business and management academics. *Human Resource Development International*, 4: 438–458.

Mullins, G. and Kiley, M. (2002) 'It's a PhD, not a Nobel Prize': How experienced examiners assess research theses. *Studies in Higher Education*, 27(4): 369–386.

Nygaard, L. (2015) *Writing for Scholars: A Practical Guide to Making Sense and Being Heard* (2nd edition). London: Sage.

Pástor, A. and Wakeling, P. (2018) All PhDs are equal but . . . Institutional and social stratification in access to the doctorate. *British Journal of Sociology of Education*, 39(7): 982–997.

Peacock, S. (2017) The PhD by publication. *International Journal of Doctoral Studies*, 12: 123–134.

Petre, M. and Rugg, G. (2010) *The Unwritten Rules of PhD Research*. Maidenhead: Open University Press.

Phillips, E.M. and Pugh, D.S. (2015) *How to Get a PhD: A Handbook for Students and their Supervisors*. Buckingham: Open University Press.

Rainer, T. (1978) *The New Diary: How to Use a Journal for Self Guidance and Expanded Creativity*. London: Angus and Robertson.

Rees, S., Ousey, K., Koo, K., Ahmad, N. and Bowling, F.L. (2019) Higher degrees in nursing: Traditional research PhD or professional doctorate? *British Journal of Nursing*, 28(14): 940–945.

REF (2019) *Guidance on Submissions*. Available at: https://www.ref.ac.uk/media/1092/ref-2019_01-guidance-on-submissions.pdf (accessed 6 May 2020).

Resnik, D.B. (2015) Bioethical issues in providing financial incentives to research participants. *Medicolegal and Bioethics*, 5: 35–41.

Skakni, I. (2018) Reasons, motives and motivations for completing a PhD: A typology of doctoral studies as a quest. *Studies in Graduate and Postdoctoral Education*, 9(5): 197–212.

Skills You Need (n.d.) *Template SWOT Analysis Personal SWOT Analysis*. Available at: www.skillsyouneed.com/ps/personal-swot-analysis.html (accessed 15 December 2019).

VITAE (2010a) *Researcher Development Framework*. Available at: https://www.vitae.ac.uk/researchers-professional-development/about-the-vitae-researcher-development-framework/developing-the-vitae-researcher-development-framework (accessed 15 September 2020).

VITAE (2010b) *Researcher Development Framework Planner*. Available at: https://www.vitae.ac.uk/researchers-professional-development/about-the-vitae-researcher-development-framework-planner (accessed 15 September 2020).

Vodde, R. and Giddings, M. (2000) The Field System Eco-map: A tool for conceptualizing practicum experiences. *Journal of Teaching in Social Work*, 20(3/4): 41–61.

Volkert, D., Candelab, L. and Bernackic, M. (2018) Student motivation, stressors, and intent to leave nursing doctoral study: A national study using path analysis. *Nurse Education Today*, 61: 210–215.

Wildy, H., Peden, S. and Chan, K. (2015) The rise of professional doctorates: Case studies of the doctorate in education in China, Iceland and Australia. *Studies in Higher Education*, 40(5): 761–774.

Williams, S. (2019) *Postgraduate Research Experience Survey*. London: Advance HE.

Wisker, G. (2008) *The Postgraduate Research Handbook* (2nd edition). Basingstoke: Palgrave Macmillan.

Index

Page numbers in *italics* refer to figures; page numbers in **bold** refer to tables.